PAUL'S KITE

By the same author

Ruth Crane
River Song
At Willie Tucker's Place
Leaving Home

PAUL'S KITE

Alison Morgan

1981

CHATTO & WINDUS

LONDON

Published by
Chatto & Windus Ltd, 40 William IV Street
London WC2N 4DF

Clarke, Irwin & Co. Ltd
Toronto

© Alison Morgan 1981

British Library Cataloguing in Publication Data

Morgan, Alison
Paul's kite
I. Title
823'.914[J]   PZ7

ISBN 0 7011 2594 2

Printed in Great Britain by
Ebenezer Baylis & Son, Ltd
The Trinity Press, Worcester, and London

To Wendy

1

Paul stood on the platform at the railway station with Mrs Dawkes and Joanna, waiting for the train to come in. He wished it would be quick. When his aunt had told him that he could travel up to London alone, because if she put him on the train at this end and his mother met him at the other, nothing could go wrong, he had accepted the arrangement as a matter of course. But he had never been on a station platform in his life, so was not prepared for the bustle and noise and sense of unease that pervades such places.

'Is Paddington as big as this?' he asked.

'Oh, much bigger,' said his aunt. 'But all you have to do is walk along the platform to the big square place at the end and stand by the Departure Board, and your mother will be there to meet you.' She explained once more exactly what the Departure Board looked like, and told him he could ask any official if he was not sure.

'There are hundreds and hundreds of platforms,' said Joanna, 'and taxis drive around right in the station, and trolleys with luggage, and there are shops and people selling things to eat and it's *terribly* noisy. And there are millions of people, all running and shouting.'

Mrs Dawkes looked down at her nephew's set face and wished she had not allowed herself to be persuaded by her husband that Paul could manage on his own. But there were those important investigations Mr Dawkes had to attend this morning and she knew he wanted her at home when he got back.

'How will Paul recognise his mother?' Joanna asked. 'If she's not a bit like you?'

'She is a *bit* like; anyway, she'll know Paul. There

1

won't be that number of eleven-year-old boys looking for someone.'

'Paul ought to have a notice round his neck saying "Paul",' said Joanna. Like a calf at the market, thought Paul, stamped with the buyer's mark. He did not trust himself to say much, but there was one question he had to ask.

'What happens if she's not there?' he said.

'Here's the train!' shouted Joanna.

'Go to the enquiries place and explain what's happened. They'll help you ring up. Remember, you've got her telephone number, and ours. But don't worry about that. She'll be there all right.' The train was already in the station and people were climbing out, and climbing in. Mrs Dawkes just had time to plant a quick kiss on Paul's cold forehead and bundle him in before the porters came by slamming doors shut. She tried to signal to him how to open the window so that they could go on talking, but he was still struggling when the train moved out.

He sat down on the seat, feeling as though there was nothing but a great hollow inside him, stretching from the pit of his stomach to the back of his throat. His hold-all was on the seat beside him, and he clutched it tightly.

Six months ago all the world that Paul had known was a green valley folded away in the Welsh hills, a cottage with no road to it, water that had to be caught in the kettle from where it spilled out of a makeshift pipe outside the back door, and an old man with three goats and a few chickens waiting to welcome him when he trudged home from school. Then the old man, his grandfather, had died, and that small, safe, happy world vanished for ever.

Strange relations whom he had never heard of had appeared from nowhere and whisked him away to a smart house on the outskirts of a seaside town sixty miles away. The woman turned out to be his Auntie Jean; she had a husband whom it seemed Paul must call Uncle William, though he did not feel like an uncle at all. He put on a jolly voice when he spoke to Paul, but tried to avoid being with him whenever possible; Paul would have preferred to call him Mr Dawkes, or Sir, like a schoolteacher. Then there was Joanna, his cousin, six weeks younger than Paul.

Auntie Jean had been kind and had tried to make him feel at home, but Paul knew that as soon as his grandfather died, everybody had begun to hunt around frantically for his parents, about whom Paul knew little and cared less. His mother had run off with another man when he was scarcely more than a baby, so he saw no reason to care about her. His father had moved away, looking for work, and left Paul in the care of his grandparents on the tiny hill farm where they had always lived. Paul remembered his grandmother with affection; she had been small and warm and always busy. She never spoke to him about his mother, but he could still recall the hardness in her voice when answering some neighbours' questions about her; and she always sighed when she took down the old framed school photograph of her son to dust it. When she died, there was much talk about how her son would surely come home for his mother's funeral, but he never came, and people said he must be dead. Grandmother had an address she used to write to before she became ill, but Paul had only a hazy recollection, when he was very young, of her ever getting a letter back; he remembered her reading it aloud, following the lines with her finger, but what was in it he had no idea. Grandad wrote to him twice, once when she became ill and once when she died; Paul remembered that because he was eight at the time, and those were the only occasions on which he

3

ever saw his grandfather write a letter.

He would have quite liked to discover his father, for the talk at the funeral had awakened his interest, but it was his mother who had turned up. At least, she had telephoned her sister, soon after Paul went to live with Auntie Jean. The police had traced her and told her what had happened, but she had never bothered to come down from London to see him. So why was he being bundled off in the train like this to stay with her, perhaps even to live with her? Life with his uncle and aunt had not been happy, because it was so different from the old world of his childhood, and he missed his grandfather, but he was just beginning to get used to it. Besides, there was Joanna, who had frightened him at first, with her clothes and books and records, her ballet classes and her quick, confident ways; but she had been a good friend to him when he had got into trouble with his uncle, and he found himself wishing she was here on the train with him.

He clutched his hold-all closer to him; it was all, now, he could call his own. He sat like a castaway on a desert island, for the other people in the carriage meant no more to him than rocks or sand. He felt very lonely.

'Is this seat taken, then?' said a wheezy voice by his ear, and he swung round, startled. There, puffing and smirking, was Grandpa.

'No,' said Paul, the colour flooding into his face, almost sick as the tide of relief surged through the empty cavern inside him. Grandpa was not the loved old man who had brought Paul up on the little hill farm; Grandpa was Auntie Jean's father, who lived a dull life in an old people's home. Paul had only met him once, when he had gone with his aunt and Joanna to take him out for a day by the sea. He was grubby and wicked and cheerful, and he treated Paul like a companion, as Grandad had done, not as the tiresome small boy that

4

Uncle William seemed to think he was. He seized the hold-all and looked for somewhere to put it that would give Grandpa room to sit.

'Up there,' said Grandpa, and Paul saw the luggage rack above. 'Surprised to see me?' he went on, settling himself comfortably as Paul struggled with the heavy bag.

'Very,' said Paul. He looked down on the old man as he stood on the seat and jammed the hold-all safely in place. Then he jumped down and sat beside him, and put his hand on the knobbly knuckles resting on the baggy trouser knees. 'Do you often come on this train?' he asked.

'First time in fifteen year, I reckon,' said the old man.

'Did you know I'd be on it?'

'Of course. Why else do you think I'm here?'

'But . . . Auntie Jean never said.'

'She wouldn't, would she, seeing as she wasn't to know, was she? And don't you go telling her, neither, or there'll be the devil to pay.'

'You didn't come just to keep me company, did you?'

'As I see it, it's more a matter of you keeping me company,' said the old man. 'I'm getting too old to travel on my own, I reckon.' He coughed, as if to prove it, and disappeared for a long time behind a large, dirty handkerchief making horrible noises, while Paul watched the landscape unroll and glowed with affection for the old man beside him. Perhaps he cast a glance too revealing at his companion's deplorable clothing, because when Grandpa finally emerged from the handkerchief and got his breath back, he said, 'Couldn't come properly dressed for travel, or Matron would have guessed something was up.'

'Doesn't she know you've come, either?'

'Not likely. She'd have locked me in my room.'

'Really?'

'Chained me to my bed, most like. Terrible woman, terrible woman.' Paul surveyed him seriously, and Grandpa, meeting his glance, said, 'Do you believe everything I say?'

'No,' said Paul. 'Not quite.' They both laughed. After a while, Paul asked, 'Is she expecting you . . . your daughter?'

'Your mum, you mean? No, she isn't expecting me. Leastways, I shouldn't think so. I haven't set eyes on her for twelve year. Once, after she married, she came to see me. That was for my old woman's funeral, your grandmother that would have been.'

'Was I born then?'

'No, but not far off. There they were at the funeral, your mother and your Auntie Jean, both like ships in full sail, and your grandmother never lived to see either of her grandchildren. Pity, that was.'

'She never knew about my mother running off, then, either, did she?' said Paul.

'You blame her for that, shouldn't wonder,' said Grandpa, and sighed. 'But you're going to stay with her now, for all that.'

'I haven't much choice, have I?'

'She were too pretty to go and lose herself up in the mountains. Spoilt her, we did, I suppose. But she was lovely. Should have married a prince of the realm, I reckon. My old woman used to say that Megan could twist me round her little finger when she were a toddler. She was right, too; and she weren't much better herself.'

'Did you spoil Auntie Jean, too?'

'Don't remember about her so much. But Megan, now, she had a way with her. She'll be at the station to meet you, I suppose?'

'Is that why you've come, to see her again?'

Grandpa said, 'Could be; could be some part of it, let's be honest.' And he coughed and wheezed in

6

thought, while the train swayed on its way to London.

'She's never done nothing for you,' said Paul, and he thought of his Auntie Jean. Uncle William had grumbled when she took the children to visit Grandpa, and though Grandpa had liked seeing them, he had never said 'Thank you' to Auntie Jean.

'I don't need nothing done for me,' said Grandpa. 'I got too many women doing that. I just want to see her again, just see her, that's all, at the railway station; then I'll take the next train back home.'

'Is that all?' said Paul. 'Go all the way up to London and straight back home again, just to see her at the station?'

'That's all,' said Grandpa. 'I don't expect her to ask me to her home. Posh place, it'll be, if I know anything about my Megan. Not the kind of place where I'd fit in.' He picked at a grease-spot on his trousers with a bulbous finger.

'What about me?' said Paul. Grandpa screwed round slowly in his seat to look Paul over.

'You'll be all right,' he said. 'You can trust Jean to fit you up nice and tidy, I'll say that for her.' Paul was not really thinking about his clothes. He was wondering how he himself would fit in at a posh place in London.

'Perhaps she'll ask you as well, when she sees you've come all the way,' he said, hopefully.

'I wouldn't bank on it,' said Grandpa.

When at last the train left the rolling countryside behind and began to cut through the mile upon mile of suburbs on the last stage of their journey, Grandpa began to show signs of nervousness. He scratched at the spots on his jacket, fiddled with his tie, ran a shaky hand over his wisps of hair, and asked Paul to help him along the corridor to the toilet. Paul was terribly afraid that the train would pull into the station while they were there, and go out again before he could get the old man

7

back to their seats and his luggage, and wished he had thought about it earlier. But the roofs and streets went on and on, and Paul still had time to watch them go by from his seat before they pulled into Paddington.

Grandpa may have got onto the train by himself, or so he had assured Paul, but he was unbearably slow and shaky getting off again, and had to stop and puff every so often as they made their way up the long platform, jostled and overtaken by the urgent crowds. Paul began to worry that his mother would have given them up and gone away before they ever reached the Departure Board, but when Grandpa showed that he, too, was worried about this and suggested Paul should run ahead and leave him to catch up at his own pace, Paul found he was much more afraid of losing Grandpa than of missing his mother, so they stuck together.

Whenever they saw a blonde young woman among the scurrying crowds, Grandpa would say, 'That's her; no, no, no it's not; too old.' Or, 'She's taller than that,' or, 'Not so fat – look for a girl with a beautiful figure.' But when Paul drew his attention to a likely person, he would say, 'No, no, nothing like that at all. That's a middle-aged woman, Paul.' Paul expected his mother to look middle-aged, like Auntie Jean.

But under the Departure Board, when they eventually reached it, there were no blonde women waiting, young or old. There were a smart, tall, young African, an old lady with white hair, and a stout man in a raincoat; these all eventually found the people they were looking for, or drifted away, and one or two others took their place, but no one who could possibly be Paul's mother. Paul found the presence of his grandpa a great comfort at this stage.

'She'll be along soon, don't you worry,' he said. 'She was never what you'd call punctual.' But when nearly half an hour had passed, even he began to show his doubts, and told Paul to nip round and see if there were any similar notice boards.

'You'll stay here, won't you?' said Paul, and although his grandpa assured him that he wouldn't move, Paul kept glancing back as he wove through the people, reassuring himself with the sight of the shabby old man sitting on the bench, hands clasped over the knob of his stick. A youngish man with ginger hair was pacing about nearby, looking restless. He caught Paul's eye and seemed to be in two minds about waving to him, but a trolley loaded with mail bags rattled between them and Paul moved on.

He was startled, then, a few moments later, to feel a hand on his arm and see the young man standing beside him.

'I say,' he said, 'are you Paul?'

'Yes,' said Paul.

'I'm a friend of your mother's. I've been looking for you – I was afraid I must have missed you.'

'I was waiting for my mother under that board.'

'I saw you. But you were with that old man, so I thought it couldn't be you.' They were walking back towards Grandpa. 'She said you'd be on your own.'

'Where's my mother?'

'She couldn't make it. She asked me to come instead.' Paul stopped dead, but his grandpa had seen him and was waving excitedly and pointing at a beautiful smartly-dressed woman in a fur coat, with golden hair piled high on her head. 'Quick!' he said, as soon as Paul got near enough. 'That's her. You've just missed her; run and catch her up.'

'No,' said Paul. 'That can't be her. She's not coming.' The woman met up with a man carrying two suitcases, and together they passed through the ticket barrier and made for a waiting train.

'Not coming?' said Grandpa, and his eyes took in the

ginger-haired man. His whole frame seemed to sag, and he looked shabbier than ever.

'Who's this?' said the ginger man to Paul.

'I'm his grandpa,' the old man answered, for him. 'Thought I'd just pop up on the train with him to see he got here safely.' His eyes met Paul's, for a moment, and he went on, in a hearty tone, 'The boy's not used to travelling. I thought he'd like a bit of company.'

'Ah,' said the man. 'Pleased to meet you.' He shook hands. 'My name's Ian,' he added, and stood, wondering what to do next.

'Friend of Megan's, are you?' asked Grandpa.

'That's right. Do you know her?'

'I ought to.' Grandpa began to laugh, but it turned into one of his coughing fits. Ian looked away in distaste.

'Megan's his daughter,' said Paul. 'My mother, you know.'

'He's Megan's father?' said Ian. He surveyed the old man for a while. 'I didn't know she'd got one,' he added, foolishly. 'We ought to push off, you know. We're late already, and I've got an appointment myself I must get to as soon as I've dumped you on Megan.'

'Can he come too? He hasn't seen her for a long time.' Grandpa was mopping up after the worst of the bout had passed, and listening.

'Hardly,' said Ian. He turned to the old man. 'She'll be ever so sorry she missed you,' he said. 'If she'd known you were coming. . . .' he trailed off. 'She's working, you, see, this morning. Got a session with the photographers.'

'Got a job, has she?' asked Grandpa. 'What does she do, then?'

'Oh, modelling, for fashion magazines, some dress shows, that sort of thing.'

'One of your top models, is she?' said Grandpa.

10

'That's my Megan, down to the ground.'

'She doesn't do so much as she used to,' said Ian.

'D'you hear that?' said Grandpa. 'Top model, eh? I'll have to get your Auntie Jean to get me all these smart magazines. "That's my daughter," I'll be able to say to Matron. That'll put her in her place, the old bag.'

'I don't think you'll find her in the nationals,' said Ian. 'Very competitive world, fashion modelling. We must be getting along. Sorry I can't take you to the flat, Mr . . . ? I don't know when Megan will be getting home. I'll be leaving Paul at the studio where she's working this morning.'

'Can't Grandpa come too?' Paul asked again.

'See me in a fashion place like that?' said Grandpa. 'I've got to get back anyhow.' He looked up at the Departure Board under which they had been waiting for so long. 'Can you find me a train on that thing, Mister?' he asked.

He had just missed one train, Ian told him. The next one would be leaving from Platform Nine in an hour's time.

'What'll you do?' said Paul.

'Just sit here quiet till it's due.'

'It's a long time,' said Paul.

'It's all I'd be doing back at the Home,' said Grandpa. 'All of us, sitting in rows, waiting to be dusted once in a while. You gets used to sitting. Tell you what, though, boy. Could you just fetch me a cup of tea from one of them trolleys before you go?'

'We really haven't time,' began Ian, but Paul waited patiently while Grandpa fumbled in his pockets for some change.

'*I'll* get it, then,' said Ian. 'It'll be quicker.' And he was back with the steaming cardboard cup before Grandpa had got the money out.

'How much do I owe you?' asked Grandpa, but Ian

11

said it didn't matter, and they must be off. He seized Paul's bag and swung away across the platform, and Paul only had time for a hurried goodbye before trotting after him.

'I hope he'll be all right,' he said, looking back.

'I don't know why he couldn't wait and get his tea after we'd gone,' said the young man. 'It would have helped fill up the time.'

'He wouldn't have been able to carry it back without spilling it,' said Paul. He felt aggrieved and angry on Grandpa's behalf, yet didn't know who to blame.

They travelled by Underground. Paul found the echoing crowded tunnels numbing and yet exciting, and he stared in wonder down the dark holes from which the lighted trains emerged. The sough of the sliding doors, and the rumble of unseen trains in other tunnels, the dipping lights that shone on the shiny knobs hanging from the ceiling, the kaleidoscope of faces, some vacant, some absorbed, the jostling advertisements, the grimy ribbed floors, all beat upon his consciousness with their strangeness so that by the time he emerged on a London pavement he was too dazed to take in any more than a jumbled impression of shops and traffic that might have been in any big town.

Ian was plainly fretting about the time. He kept looking at his watch, and walking faster and faster, dodging between the crowds, so that Paul feared he would lose him. Then he suddenly stopped by a door between two shop fronts and said, 'It's up there. Straight up the stairs, second door on the left.' He pushed the door open for Paul to walk in.

'Aren't you coming?' said Paul, panic-stricken.

'Sorry, I'm late already. You'll be all right. You can't miss it. See you later.' He let the door swing to and Paul found himself standing alone in a dark well at the bottom of a narrow flight of stairs.

If he had known how to do it, Paul would have walked straight back to the Underground and taken the next train to Paddington, hoping to find Grandpa still waiting. Instead, he stumped doggedly up the stairs, and knocked on the second door on the left.

There was a lot of talking and movement going on and Paul's knock went unheard. He tried again and then, in desperation, started to open the door. Somebody was evidently leaning against it, because it opened about an inch and swung shut again. A moment later it opened again, from inside, about three inches this time, and a face appeared in the crack. 'What do you want?' asked the man, a plump, short figure in a brightly coloured shirt.

'I was told to come here,' said Paul. 'I'm Paul Evans.'

'Sorry,' said the man. 'Wrong room. Or wrong date. There's no kids' session today.' He began to close the door.

'I'm meeting my mother here,' said Paul.

'Oh? Which one's she?'

'Mrs Evans.' The man looked blank. 'She's expecting me.'

'What's her other name? First name?'

'Megan.'

The man turned away to speak to an unseen neighbour. The room appeared to be full of people waiting about, mostly women, as far as Paul could see through the sliver of doorway. 'Anyone here called Megan?' the man asked. He turned back to Paul. 'What's she like?' he said.

Paul opened his mouth to say that he didn't know, but to his shame he found his lip trembling, and a horrible tight feeling at the back of his throat. But it was dark where he stood, and the man noticed nothing. 'Oh, yeah,' he said. 'She's here. Norma knows her. You better have a word with him, Norma.' He opened the

13

door slightly wider, and Paul could see that beyond the crowded nearer end of the room was a tangle of cables and lights and cameras, and beyond that again an area almost like a stage, all lit up, where two women in bobble hats and thick pullovers stood, one holding a pair of skis, the other a toboggan.

'She'll come in a minute,' a dark young woman said in Paul's ear. 'As you can see, she's in session at the moment.' Someone shouted, 'O.K.' and both the bobble-hatted women began to grin ecstatically at a dirty mark on the wall as the camera clicked.

Paul wanted to ask which one was his mother, but did not like to display his ignorance. In any case, under the bright lights and heavy make-up and bobble hats, they both looked alike to him.

'You'd beter wait outside,' said the plump man. 'Norma'll tell her you're here. Won't you, Norma?'

'When she's through,' said Norma. She looked at Paul. 'You her kid?' Paul nodded. 'Didn't know she had any. Nephew, she told me. How old are you?'

'Twelve, nearly.'

Norma exchanged a glance with the plump man, and laughed. 'That'd put a few years on our Megan,' she said. 'You wait in the corridor, there's a love, and your mum or your auntie or whoever she is will be along directly.'

Paul found himself back at the dark stair-head. He sat on the top step and rested his forehead on his knees; he had not let the tears come while he was in the bright room, and he did not want them to shame him now, in case his mother should arrive – or his auntie, or whoever she was. Why had she told them that?

When he opened his eyes there was nothing to see but walls and closed doors, a narrow passage and a narrow stairway, and one window, high up, through which he could see another wall. That was all London seemed to

14

be: a place without sky. First Paddington, then the Underground, then here. The quick scurry through the streets had not given him time to do more than keep his eyes on Ian's figure cutting through the crowds ahead of him. It would be exciting visiting London, Auntie Jean had told him.

He closed his eyes and tried to imagine himself back on the hill farm with Grandad, among the chickens, the three goats and a handful of sheep. Each had its own particular smell, and feel; the greasy curled wool of the sheep, tough on their heaving flanks when you held them and they stared at you with panicky eyes. The goats' hair was coarse and dry, and you could run your finger up through it, feeling every bone along the knobbly spine, for the goats were tame and trusting as dogs; they pressed against you, unafraid, asking you to scratch them between the horns that thrust up, strong and hard, from the temples.

Davy, Paul's own pet goat, loved particularly to be scratched in this way, or to let Paul wrestle with him, grasping the horns in his two hands. Then Paul would lie on the cropped turf to get his breath back, the smells of bracken and mountain earth sharp in his nostrils, and the water-music of the brook always in his ears. It was like a clock, that brook; sometimes loud and incessant, and at other times you did not notice it at all, and yet it never stopped. In another way, it was not like a clock at all, for a clock always keeps the same regular tick-tock, but the stream had a hundred different tunes to play, sometimes shouting, sometimes whispering, sometimes slow as a day-dream, sometimes roaring by in a thunderous haste.

Now Davy was dead. Paul could never think about Davy without pain. The other animals had been sold or given away, but Davy was dead. Paul had not forgiven Uncle William for that, for not finding room for Davy

15

in his neat suburban garden, so that Davy, too old to find a new home, had had to be destroyed. Perhaps if it had not been for Uncle William and Davy, Paul would have settled happily enough in his new home in Port Mynach with his relations, instead of being bundled off to stay with his unknown and unloved mother.

Davy was gone, along with the sheep and chickens, along with Grandad. The stream still made music, but not for Paul's ears. Someone different now lived in the little cottage on the hill. . . . Paul's thoughts took a happier turn, for no-one could think of Mr Abraham without feeling a little bit more cheerful. He was actually a retired judge, and had all kinds of important-sounding titles, but Mr Abraham was how Paul thought of him. He had first called him that because he had not realised Abraham was just his Christian name, but it had stuck.

When Paul first came across him, he had been up on the roof of the old cottage making a skylight, all by himself, so that he could watch for Unidentified Flying Objects, and Paul had been running away from the new home in Port Mynach. Paul couldn't exactly claim that Mr Abraham had made him go back – and yet, after talking to Mr Abraham, Paul had found that he had made up his mind himself that he must do just that. It hadn't made the going back any easier, though. I suppose, thought Paul sadly, it was because of me running away that Uncle William and Auntie Jean decided I must go and live with my mother after all. That, and because the family was planning a holiday in Spain and didn't want to have to take Paul with them. Nobody really wants me, he thought, not even old Grandpa, or Mr Abraham. They liked him well enough, but they were both old men and not able to look after him. As for his mother – she had not wanted to have him; she had not met him at the station, she had not come now to speak to him, apparently she had not even

16

claimed him as her son to the people she worked with.

He ran his finger-nail up and down the shining zip on his hold-all, listening to the sound. If he did it slowly, he could make a ticking noise, but it was hard to get it even, like a watch. It wasn't much of an occupation, but it was better than letting his mind run free.

But one cannot anchor one's mind to a zip-fastener for ever. Soon Paul's thoughts had gone galloping away again, and in an unexpected direction, to Uncle William. Uncle William had a nine-to-five job, like every other man in the road where they lived. He worked for an insurance company, though what that meant Paul had no idea. At home – his old, proper home – you could see people going about their work all day; as he walked back from school he would talk to the farmer laying a hedge alongside the lane, or the road-men who, as often as not, were gouging out the hedges with their great machines to straighten a sharp bend. He knew all the forestry workers, the whine of whose chainsaws echoed from the wooded hills, and sometimes cadged a lift in the grocer's delivery van. The school-teacher, village postmistress, garage mechanic, were working around him all day; you could see what *they* did for a living, but Uncle William, once he had left the house at ten to nine every morning simply disappeared out of Paul's world until he returned in the evening. Not that Paul minded; life was much more comfortable when Uncle William was out.

It was not until Paul overheard a conversation between Uncle William and Auntie Jean one evening when he was supposed to be asleep in bed, that he ever gave a single thought to what Uncle William did when he wasn't at home. Paul's bedroom window overlooked the flat roof of the kitchen, and one hot summer night when he couldn't sleep he had climbed out onto it, and could hear his uncle and aunt talking in the living-room

17

below, through the open window. Uncle William, it seemed, was very worried about an inspection that was to take place at his office, and Auntie Jean was trying to cheer him up, saying it wasn't his fault if there was some kind of trouble. Paul got the impression it was something to do with money, but he couldn't be sure, now, whether either of them had actually mentioned money. Two men had come to the house to see Uncle William earlier that evening, and that was unusual, too; and it was because of that inspection that Auntie Jean had not been able to come up to London with Paul today, though for the life of him Paul couldn't imagine what it had got to do with her.

The funny thing about that night was that Uncle William had sounded so anxious, and Auntie Jean so firm and strong. Usually it was the other way about. Peering cautiously down from the roof to make sure they could not see him, he had been able to make out Uncle William sitting in his chair with his back to Paul, and Auntie Jean perched on the arm, one hand on her husband's shoulder, the other holding his hand reassuringly. Paul had slipped away quietly, but the scene had lingered in his mind because of its unexpectedness.

Later that same evening, Uncle William had shown another unexpected side to his nature, standing out in the moonlit garden taking great delight in watching Paul's hedgehog, Prickles, scuttling round the garden devouring slugs. Prickles was an unexpected bonus – Paul had come upon him injured in the lane while he was staying with Mr Abraham. Paul was very doubtful about bringing Prickles back to live with the Dawkes's, even though hedgehogs are good for gardens and Uncle William loved his garden, but now it seemed Uncle William really did like having the little hedgehog around. Indeed, before Paul left for London, Uncle William had built him a sort of Hedgehog Palace in the rockery. He makes a home for Prickles, but not for me, thought Paul, running his finger so violently along the zip-fastener that it hurt.

The door opened, and his mother stood there. At least, he supposed she must be his mother. She still wore the absurd heavy sweater, but she had taken off the bobble hat and her hair clung damply to her forehead above the mask of make-up, so that she looked like two people put together.

'Paul!' she said. 'My darling.'

'Hullo,' said Paul. He did not know whether to talk to the beautiful bronzed mask or the rather scruffy-looking head.

'Isn't this marvellous?' she said. 'Fancy seeing you after all these years! Sorry I couldn't meet you at the station, but Ian found you all right, I'm sure. Now, I was hoping I'd be finished, but they are going to want me for another couple of hours, I'm afraid, so what I'm going to suggest is, that I give you some money and you can go and get yourself something to eat and have a look round, and meet me here at —' she looked at her watch — 'say, five o'clock. It's just coming up to three now.' She held out a pound note to him.

'It's all right,' said Paul. 'Grandpa and I had some sandwiches on the train. He came up to see you.' He did not take the money. He did not want her money and he was afraid to go out into the world of London.

'Grandpa? That old man? Whatever for?'

'To see you.'

'My father? I thought he was in an old people's home.'

'He is. He wanted to see you. He said he hadn't seen you since before I was born. He thought you'd be at the station to meet me.'

Megan looked anxious. 'What have you done with him? He's not here, is he?'

'He took the next train home.'

19

'Thank goodness for that. We can't have him wandering around London at his age. Whatever was Jean thinking, to let him come without telling me?'

'She didn't know,' began Paul, but his mother interrupted him.

'You must tell me all about the family this evening, darling. I've got to go back and get cleaned up for the next one. Isn't it ridiculous, having to wear these great thick things in July? That's modelling for you.' Paul had always thought that modelling was making up little plastic tanks and aeroplanes, and said nothing. Megan pushed the pound note at him. 'Take it, quick,' she said. 'I must go. Don't forget. Five o'clock. Down on the street would be best.'

'What happens if I get lost?' said Paul.

'Don't,' said his mother, as if that settled it, and was gone, leaving Paul alone on the stairs again, with a pound note in his hand. He had five more in his pocket that Auntie Jean had given him. He had never had so much money in his life.

He walked slowly down the stairs and out into the street. The air was bright as gold after the dim stairway and he stood for a moment, blinking like a cat. Cars were parked all along his side of the street, each nuzzling at a meter like cows in their milking stalls. A pigeon jerked along the kerb, not two yards from him, pecking here and there for unseen food, its feet pink and clean-looking in surprising contrast to its grimy feathers. He looked at the shop windows on each side of the door, and at others up and down the street. They were not the kind of shops to which he was accustomed, selling groceries and plastic buckets and check shirts for farmers and trim suits for farmers' wives; these shops mostly seemed to sell brochures about foreign countries or insurance, though one had a single gold-framed picture in the window, and another a stuffed bear, an

20

enormous pot-plant and a drum.

He walked carefully down the street, remembering this was the way he had come with Ian, counting the side-roads as he crossed them until he emerged on a much wider, busier road. Here the sun poured down even more brightly, and the scarlet buses cast fleeting shadows on him as they passed. The pavements were crowded again and he could see people coming and going at the entrance of the Underground like wasps from their papery nest in a disused rabbit hole on just such a sunny July day as this.

On the corner where he stood was a newsagent's; on the opposite corner, a café. He crossed the road in the shelter of a family of Indians, and peered in at the café window. It was a self-service place, such as he had been to once, years ago, when he had gone with his grand-mother on a coach trip to the pantomime; but after she died, he went to the pub with his grandad on market days, nowhere else. He was not hungry enough to dare to go in; anyhow, there was plenty of time. He walked on down the street, and found it full of eating places; some of them had menus on the door, and he was shocked at the prices. There were also other shops, proper shops, though still quite different from those in his market town back home: shops that sold nothing but umbrellas, or Persian carpets, or conjuring tricks; Paul spent a long time at that window, studying the false noses and joke inkstains and comic balloons; another was full of garden gnomes and another sold all kinds of Indian carved things. Suddenly he came upon a shop that sold nothing but ice-creams, over thirty different varieties it said above the door. He went in, and stared at the glass-fronted cases displaying ice-cream in quantities as well as varieties that he had never dreamed of. The trouble was, he could not make up his mind which to have. He hung about, watching other people come in and buy single cones, or double deckers, or triple deckers, or tubs of various kinds, until there was a lull, and nobody was in the shop but him. He stared nervously at the large woman behind one of the counters; her hair was piled in a golden splendour of curls high above her head like one of her own ice-cream cones, and Paul thought she looked very smart and alarming.

'What's it to be, ducky?' she said.

'I don't know,' said Paul. 'There's too many; difficult to choose, it is.'

'Indeed to goodness, you're a long way from home,' said the lady, and her face creased into a cheery grin full of big white teeth. 'What part of Wales do you come from?'

'Bwlchywern,' said Paul, but she was none the wiser. 'How do you know I come from Wales?'

'I married a Welshman,' said the lady. 'All his relations talk like you. Been in London long?'

'Only about an hour,' said Paul.

'Ah,' said the lady. 'If you're not in a hurry, I'll just serve this lady first —' someone had come into the shop — 'and then I'll tell you what they're all like.'

She was as good as her word. She took him on a voyage of exploration up and down the containers, the tangerines, lime-greens, dark chocolates and coffees, pinks and violets and a host of others, spotted, striped, streaked, blotched, some silky-smooth, others full of nuts or bits of toffee or chopped fruits that gleamed like jewels. He eventually left the shop licking a gigantic triple decker generously topped with a variety of sauces, sixty pence the poorer but richer for having found a friend.

He wandered on down the street, enjoying his ice-cream, and when it was finished, he wandered back again until he came to the turning from which he had first come. Then he walked up the street the other way,

22

till he came to a great meeting place of roads, with a complicated maze of traffic lights, pedestrian crossings and one-way streets. Everything – people and cars – seemed to be obeying some code of rules, but the rules were too complicated for Paul. He put a hesitant foot over the kerb and was nearly blown backwards as a bus swept by a few inches from his face. He decided to follow the next turning to his left, so that he could carry on walking without crossing any roads; perhaps, if he walked far enough, and turned left again, he would find himself back where he started.

When, in due course, he found he had done just that, he felt as proud as Columbus. He had conquered one small section of this great city. He had no idea where his little patch fitted into the overall map of the capital, but if ever he found himself here again, he would be at home.

He walked round the triangle again, and this time he was able to time himself, because he found a watch and clock shop on his route. It took him ten minutes, and that included waving at the lady with the golden curls. A traffic warden was walking up his street, reading the meters and jotting things down in a little notebook, and when he came round and in at the top, he met the same warden, still at his job, higher up. He began to feel like an old resident. The same pigeon was there, too; or was it a different one? It was as tame as a farmyard hen.

He still had nearly an hour to fill in, and now that he had established his bearings he became bolder, and plunged in and out of the network of tiny streets intersecting his triangle, finding much of interest – a pair of draymen lowering barrels of beer on a rope down a ramp into some kind of underground cavern; a slit in a great blank wall, through which clouds of steam kept emerging; a crazy iron fire-escape, such as he had only seen in television police series, clambering erratically to

B

a sliver of sky sandwiched between the towering blocks of masonry; an old man, unbelievably dirty, slumped against a wall in a dead end, talking to himself, watched by a dingy cat. Then there was a part where he had to walk between scaffolding poles under a sagging roof of tarpaulins and when he looked back he could see a crane rising above a wall of palings. He tried to find a way in, to see what was going on behind the palings, and eventually, after much trial and error wandering through alleys that kept leading him back to places he had been before, he did find a gateway, but it was of solid zinc and bolted on the inside. He applied one eye to a hole, and could see a bull-dozer shovelling bricks about, but then some workmen came by and went in through a smaller door set in the big one, and Paul moved away hurriedly. Whatever was going on in there was so carefully hidden, he felt he ought not to be caught trying to look.

He ran to the clock shop, and found he still had ten minutes to spare, so went boldly into the self-service café and bought himself a sausage roll and doughnut. He knew this part of London now, he was no longer shy of it. As he ambled up to the door to wait for his mother he said hullo to the traffic warden, who did not reply, and threw some crumbs for the pigeons – there were two of them now.

People began to emerge from the door. He recognised the plump man, and Norma, but not his mother, when she finally appeared. The bronzed complexion had gone along with the ski clothes. A slightish woman in slacks, with a pale face and short mousy hair said, 'Ah, there you are; had a nice time exploring, darling?' and hurried him away to the Underground.

2

Next morning, Paul woke early, roused by the unaccustomed noises of London. He lay wondering whether he should get up, and what to do if he did. The young man, Ian, had called round last evening, and was still there when Paul had gone to bed early, from a combination of tiredness, boredom and a feeling he was not really wanted. Paul did not know whether he had stayed the night and felt uncomfortable at the thought of finding him around when he got up, though he couldn't have said why he felt like that about Ian. He was quite pleasant to Paul, and had talked more to him than Megan had, but there was something about his manner that irritated Paul. He seemed to be very familiar with the flat, and with Megan, and yet at the same time very offhand with her.

The bedroom was hot and stuffy after Wales. Paul had woken in the night and thrown off most of the bed-clothes; now he kicked off the sheet and went across to look out of the window. His mother lived in a second floor flat in a row of what had once been large private houses. There were no gardens at the front, but each house had railings enclosing a short flight of steps down to a basement flat, and one or two of them had plants in pots wedged in any odd corners that were not taken up by dustbins. Under his window there were only dustbins, and a small row of milk bottles; the milk float was just down the road – it was probably the clinking of the bottles that had woken him up. A lorry rattled by, piled with scrap. Somebody came out of a door opposite, got into his car, slamming the door, and drove off with a short squeal of tyres. Some sparrows tumbled down from

25

a rooftop in a bickering cluster and began to peck about around the railings.

There were thumps coming from the floor above, which suggested that the people in that flat were getting up, but no sounds came from Megan's bedroom, next to his own. There were just the two bedrooms, kitchen and living-room and bathroom; it was quite grand and spacious compared to the little cottage he had lived in with his grandfather, but compared to his uncle and aunt's house it seemed poky; not the sort of place one would expect a top fashion model to be living in. Paul remembered Grandpa's pride in Megan's work, and Ian's unenthusiastic response. Paul knew less than nothing about fashion modelling, but it occurred to him that Megan's acquaintances in London did not give quite the same impression about the way she lived as the one her family back in Port Mynach had got.

A newspaper boy came whistling down the street with a big sack on his bicycle, sending papers skimming onto doorsteps as he passed. Paul thought it would be nice to have a job like that. He wondered if the boy came from a family full of children, with a mother who cooked breakfast for him before he went out and a father who took him to football matches on Saturdays.

His mother's bedroom door opened, and he heard noises in the kitchen. No voices, though. He decided to get dressed and see what was happening. When he emerged, he found his mother sitting in her dressing-gown painting her nails, a cup of coffee steaming beside her on the draining board.

'Hullo,' he said. 'Is it all right? I've got dressed.'

'Suit yourself,' said Megan. 'You wouldn't catch me out of bed at this time of day if I hadn't got to go to work. Make yourself a cup of coffee. There's a mug there, look.' She indicated the plate-rack, and went on with her nails.

26

Paul looked around the kitchen. Last night's supper dishes filled the sink. There was no sign of breakfast. 'I don't really like coffee,' he said. He had told her the same thing last night.

'Oh God, so you said,' remarked Megan. 'Tea-bags in that tin, there.'

Paul said, 'I'm not specially thirsty. Could I wait and have it after breakfast?'

'Oh, if you want something to *eat*,' said Megan, as though the idea was a surprise to her, 'you'll have to forage for yourself while I'm getting dressed. I'm a working woman, Paul. I can't look after you as well as your Auntie Jean did, I'm afraid.' She pointed out the bread bin and the fridge, before disappearing into her bedroom. 'You'll have to get a mid-day meal for yourself as well, today, Paul; I doubt if I'll be back much before six.'

Paul looked around the cramped kitchen, and across to the living-room, frowsty with stale tobacco smoke. 'What'll I do till you come back?' he asked.

'I don't know. What do you usually do?' Megan appeared in the doorway, buttoning up her blouse. 'There's the telly; I don't know whether any of those magazines would interest you. Tell you what, why don't you go down to the newsagent's and buy yourself a few comics? Got any money?'

Paul nodded. Megan had gone back in and was doing her hair. Paul could see her through the open door, watching herself in the mirror.

'If you come with me to the Underground,' she said, 'I'll be able to show you where the shops are, and how to get to the Park.'

'Is there a park near here, then?' That sounded more hopeful.

'Hyde Park's only ten minutes walk from here. You'll love it. There's a sandpit and some swings and things quite near-by.' Sandpits, thought Paul; how old does she think I am? That was a puzzle, for a couple of minutes later Megan was giving him a front door key, with instructions not to lose it, and various household shopping items 'maybe you would just get while you're out'. Now dressed for the world, Megan had also put on some of her conscious charm. 'Isn't it lovely for me to have a real son to be such a help to me? We're going to have such fun together, you and I.' As she hustled through, her eye was caught by the pile of dirty dishes in the sink. 'Oh, Paul, darling, I'm in such a rush today. Would you be a sweetie and just finish off those few things in the sink? It would be such a treat for me, coming back after a hard day's work, not to have that to do.'

Even with the washing-up and the shopping, it seemed a long time from breakfast to six o'clock in the evening, and his first visit to Hyde Park was disappointing. It appeared flat and dusty and crowded to a boy from the Welsh hills, and so constricted that nowhere could he get out of the sound of the traffic. Later he was to change his mind about the Park, but on that first day he saw nothing in it to excite his interest, apart from the people flying kites. He could not understand how those varied shapes, the diamonds and boxes and birds, could rise in the air so buoyantly with no hill tops to start them from and only a little wind. He did not know about the living warmth of the great city that swept them up on spiralling thermals; but he was fascinated to watch them going up and up, swooping and diving like live creatures at play. Dull and imprisoned as he felt, Paul yearned to share in their freedom and vitality. One day, he decided, he would buy a kite for himself.

During the next few weeks that Paul stayed with his mother he got to know London very well, but his mother not at all. It was not only that she looked different on every different occasion, but that she seemed to talk differently, act differently, think differently even. The only time that she was pretty much the same was at breakfast, when she wandered round in her dressing-gown drinking coffee and doing her nails, but at that time she wasn't really a person at all, being too half-awake apparently to be bothered to select a character. Then she would disappear, to keep her various appointments, leaving Paul a key so that he could come and go as he pleased. Ian reappeared, and stayed with them for some days. Paul gathered he had been living with Megan more or less all the time until recently, but now, although he treated the flat like his home, he and Megan did not spend much time together. During the day they were both at work – Ian was something called a fashion photographer, so when he and Paul's mother did have a conversation, it was all about people and things that Paul knew nothing about – and in the evenings, although they both went out a good deal, it was seldom together. Indeed, one evening, after Paul's mother had disappeared, Ian came back in with a young American woman. Paul thought her good fun, because she listened to his accounts of exploring London and persuaded Ian to play Monopoly with them. The game went on till all hours, as Monopoly will, and Ian wanted Paul to break it off and go to bed, but the girl wouldn't have it. She said she hadn't played Monopoly since she left the States, where she used to play with her kid brothers and sisters.

The next day Ian and Paul's mother were both grumpy with him as well as with each other, and went on at him because when they got back in the evening he was lounging on the settee watching the television while the sink was full of dirty dishes.

'I forgot,' said Paul. The truth was, he was tired of washing-up, and getting in groceries, and running the

29

vacuum cleaner over the carpet. He was not a lazy boy, and had suffered at his Auntie Jean's from not being allowed to do anything like that, but here, his mother was always saying, 'Just do this,' or 'Just do that,' as she was going out, and never seemed to notice that he had done it when she came back, so long as it was not there for her to do.

Various people came in, too, and would sit around drinking, smoking and talking. They never talked about anything that made any sense to Paul, and he found those evenings very boring because he could not watch the television. Sometimes his mother made a big fuss of him, trying to draw him into the conversation, and sometimes she made fun of him, and of his Welsh accent, and his farm in the hills; and sometimes she totally ignored him; it just depended upon the people she was with.

There was an older man who came quite often to take his mother out for the evening. Before his first visit, Paul's mother said to him, 'By the way, darling, I think it would be best if you called me Auntie Megan rather than Mummy, don't you?'

Paul, who had never called her anything because he could not bring himself to say any of the forms of 'mother' directly to her, said, 'Yes.' Then he added, 'Why Auntie?'

'You can make it just Megan if you'd rather,' she said. 'I'd seem more like your big sister then.'

Paul said nothing; he did not really feel that she was any relation to him at all. Given a choice, he would have addressed her as Mrs Evans. He already had an aunt, of whom he began to think more and more frequently the longer he spent with these meaningless people in London. He found himself thinking: I already have a sister, too; but then remembered Joanna was not his sister, only his cousin. Then he remembered, too, that it was they who had hustled him off to London, on his own, so that he would be out of the way while Uncle William got on with his important meetings, whatever they were, and then took his family to Spain — his family, not Paul – for a holiday. Sometimes, in the long evenings alone in Megan's flat, he would go up to the telephone and take it off its hook, summoning up courage to ring up the Dawkes family. He had the telephone number, and he read and re-read the instructions in the front of the telephone book; but in the end he always put the phone down again without making the call. If he had been sure Joanna was in, he could ask to speak to her. But he had nothing particular to say; and supposing Uncle William answered, how was he to open the conversation?

Life would have been very dismal indeed, but for two things. One was that Paul was used to spending long hours of his life without friends of his own age, having lived alone with his grandfather until the last few months, so he did not mind that so much, though it would have been fun now and again to be able to kick a football around with other boys, as he had in the school playground. The other thing was that though he felt shy and uncomfortable in the flat with all the strangers from her kind of world that Megan used to bring back, he found a new world, all his own, full of excitement. As soon as Megan slammed the flat door behind her in the morning, until at least six o'clock in the evening, he was free to explore his new world – and that world stretched from the front door as far as his legs would carry him in the time at his disposal, in whatever direction he chose to go. The flat was a foreign land to him, but the rest of London became his home.

He had long days with plenty of time and no money, and the weather was warm and fine. He set out to explore London in exactly the same way as once he had explored the Welsh hills, using his legs for transport and the sun and tall landmarks for navigation. At first, he always started by going to Hyde Park, because he knew where to find it, and though in the beginning it appeared to him as a flat and shapeless bit of grassland, he made it his own by walking over it, as he had done with the streets round the ice-cream shop on his first afternoon, until every part of it took on an especial and familiar meaning. He watched fathers and sons sailing model boats on the Round Pond, and girls giggling as they splashed about in rowing boats on the Serpentine. Then there were the grand, remote figures who passed by on horseback, living in their own superior world six feet above everybody else as they trotted and cantered by under the trees. Soon he knew where to find every statue, every wrought-iron gateway, every flower-bed, and where the family of ducklings were likely to be found. He noted, but avoided, the nannies gossiping by their prams and the young men hugging their girl friends under the trees. But he lingered, fascinated, wherever he found people flying kites. The ones with long scarlet streamers that swooped and dived were exciting, but when one caught a gust wrongly and plummeted headlong to the ground, he could scarcely bear to look, for he felt the shattering crash under his very ribs. It looked so easy to launch a kite, when he watched one going up under expert hands, that it fretted him to watch how some people – grown men as well as children – bungled and bungled it, so that the kite limped along like a lame creature, flopping to the ground time and again before it had ever really taken flight. Paul felt sure he could manage better, and longed to get his hands on the spool of twine. Most of all, he liked to lie on his back and watch a kite – often quite a small one – glide and swirl gently higher and higher till, like a lark, it was scarcely more than a speck in the sky. If I was up there, he thought, riding the kite, I could see all London, like a map. People would look like ants and buses like ladybirds, cars like woodlice and trains like caterpillars. He wondered what the Thames would look like; the curling streamer of a kite, perhaps? He had not yet seen the Thames, but he knew about the great river. Mr Abraham had told him about it – the most exciting thing in London, he had said. Auntie Jean had told him about the Houses of Parliament overlooking the river, and all the wide bridges he would cross when his mother took him sightseeing – but when would that be? She never seemed to be around to do anything with Paul, ever.

He wondered if he dared set out on the other side of Hyde Park and look for the Thames. If only he could get up like a kite, and see where everything was; but with no idea of directions or distances, he was afraid of getting lost. He found a shop that sold kites, in one of the streets between the flat and the Park. He spent a long time staring at them all, but the one he wanted would have taken all his money. One day, he told himself, he would buy it.

And then he made his big discovery. He found that he did not have to climb into the sky on the back of a kite to find his map; there was a perfectly good one quite near one of the great gateways. What was more, there was a helpful notice saying *You Are Here*, and rows of buttons which you could press and different places lit up. He spent a happy half hour lighting up all the places he had heard of, like Buckingham Palace and Madame Tussaud's, until he was disturbed by a cheery voice.

'Excuse, please. Commonwealth Institute?' Two foreigners stood there, in smart grey suits, smiling with gleaming teeth beneath small black moustaches. To Paul, they looked as alike as twins.

'I don't know,' he stammered. The two men peered along the row of buttons, and found the one they wanted. Then one of them ran a finger along the roads leading back from the light to the *You Are Here* point, reading out street names to the other, who repeated them with an air of concentration. Then they hurried off, the second man still reciting the street names.

After they had gone, Paul went back to his button-pressing, but this time with a purpose. He was looking for an interesting-sounding place that looked close enough to find without getting lost. That was how he came to spend a day at the Science Museum – where he found plenty more knobs to press. Next day he tried the Natural History Museum, and then decided he was experienced enough in map-reading to get to Bucking-ham Palace.

After that, he went everywhere. It was while he was standing among the pigeons in Trafalgar Square that a thought occurred to him. One of the properties in Monopoly was called Trafalgar Square. Another was Piccadilly, and he had been there, too.

'Are all the places in Monopoly *real*?' he asked Megan that evening, and she said yes, she supposed so. Paul got out the Monopoly board and studied it.

'Where's Whitechapel?' he asked.

'East End,' said Megan. She was doing her face at the mirror in the kitchen.

'End of what?' asked Paul. London didn't seem to *have* an end on the illuminated map. Megan had hurried into her bedroom and did not answer. Paul knew the signs. 'Are you going out tonight?' he asked.

'Well, yes, didn't I tell you? Mr Holcombe is coming to collect me, any minute now.' Paul did not say any-thing, and after a moment Megan said, 'You don't mind, do you?'

'Nuh,' said Paul, truthfully. 'Where's Vine Street?'

'It isn't that I want to go and leave you,' said Megan. 'I'd much rather have a quiet evening at home with you. It's just that Mr Holcombe has been so kind, I don't want to disappoint him. You do understand, don't you?'

'Where's Vine Street?' said Paul.

'Oh, I don't know,' said Megan, sounding suddenly cross. 'I don't believe you care whether I'm in or out.'

Paul looked up from the Monopoly board and stared at her for a moment. 'Yes I do,' he said, catching the cross note from her, and looked quickly back down to the board again. Yes, he did, he thought; life was much nicer when she was out.

Megan was scuffling about among the directories by the telephone. 'Here you are,' she said. 'Look it all up in that.' She tossed a little booklet called *London A – Z* on the table. Paul picked it up and turned the pages. Every one was covered with a maze of tiny streets, each with its name printed so small he could barely read it. None of the pages he looked at seemed to bear any relation to the bits of London he knew, and they all covered such a small square of the city that he could not see where they fitted in the general scheme of things. 'How?' he asked.

Down below, a car hooted softly. Megan parted the curtains and peered down. 'He's waiting for me,' she said. 'I must go. There's an index at the back. You work it out for yourself. It'll give you something to do while I'm out. Don't be late going to bed. Goodnight, darling.'

'Goodnight,' said Paul. He was staring at the index, but everything had gone blurred and he could not read a word of it. As soon as he heard the door shut, he dropped his head down, silently, and let the tears trickle between his fingers onto the streets of London.

It had suddenly come to him that he might have to live like this for ever. It wasn't the first time the thought had entered his head, but before it had just been a

35

thought and no more. This time it was something he felt not only in his brain but in all of him. Every bit of him ached with despair and he felt that never again would he ever spend an evening with anyone who wanted to be with him or whom he wanted to be with. The desolate thing was that he didn't care that Megan had gone out and left him alone. It would not have made any difference if she had stayed at home. He would still have been just as alone. The only person he had enjoyed talking to since he had been in London was the ice-cream lady, and perhaps that American girl. For the rest, he could be living among dead people. Most of the time he took it for granted that this was just a temporary thing; in a week or two he would go back to his uncle and aunt and Joanna, and though life there wasn't easy, at least it was real. But now this terrible thought was with him that he might never go back there, because he didn't belong to them, but to this stupid woman who happened to be his mother.

How could he get away from this place? Should he run away, back to Port Mynach where his uncle lived? Running away was something he had done before, and it hadn't solved anything. It had brought Mr Abraham into his life, though. Should he run to Mr Abraham, back to the little cottage where he had been so happy, and never known it, until his grandad died? But Mr Abraham would not think much of him for running away a second time, and anyhow, he didn't live in the cottage all year round. He was probably here in London, doing one of those important jobs he still did from time to time, although he had really retired. He didn't even know where Mr Abraham lived in London.

Perhaps he could look him up in the telephone directory, and talk to him on the phone. Paul wasn't at all sure that he was brave enough to do that, but just the idea that it could be done cheered him up enough to get up and go over to the telephone and begin turning back the pages of the directory towards *A*. *A* for *Abraham*. But of course, that wasn't his real name, only his Christian name.

As Paul let the book drop back onto the table from his disconsolate fingers, the phone suddenly pealed in his ear. The unexpectedness of it, so loud and so close, made him jump back nervously. But it went on ringing and eventually he had to pick it up, just to make it stop.

'Hullo?' he said cautiously.

'Hullo – is that Paul?'

'Yes.'

'Why, Paul, how nice to hear you. It's Auntie Jean – don't you recognise my voice?'

'Yes,' said Paul. 'I do now.' How to tell her that the sound of her voice quenched the aching loneliness like a long cold drink at the end of the weary climb up to the cottage in the hills on a hot day? He couldn't think what more to say, but he wanted her at all costs to go on talking, so that he could listen and not be alone. 'What do you want?' he said.

As soon as he had said it, he knew it sounded unfriendly from the pause at the other end.

'There's something I would like to ask Mummy, but before you get her, tell me how you are and all the things you've been doing.'

For a moment Paul couldn't think who she was talking about, but then he realised. 'Megan's out,' he said.

'Oh,' She sounded surprised.

'Can I take a message?' Paul was used to doing that by now.

Auntie Jean hesitated, then said, 'The thing is, Joanna is very keen to come and stay and see a bit of London. I was wondering whether it would be too much for your mother to have her as well as you for a few days.'

'I shouldn't think it would make much difference,' said

37

Paul, with truth. Joanna here, in London with him. That would make it like a holiday here, for him as well as for her. They could have fun together. But how would Joanna fit into this set-up? She would find it very strange. Would she enjoy it? Or make a fuss? And there was another thing. 'I thought you were going to Spain.'

'Oh, no, that's off. Didn't your mother tell you?'

'No.'

'That's odd. You must have been wondering, then, why we hadn't said any more about it to you.'

'Not particularly. It's got nothing to do with me.'

'Oh, Paul, you didn't think we'd just go without telling you, did you? You'd have been coming with us unless you'd rather have stayed with your mother. You knew that, didn't you?'

'No,' said Paul. The ice was melting inside him. 'Why aren't you going, then?'

His aunt seemed to hesitate. Then she said, 'It's because Uncle William's so busy just now, he can't get away. Joanna's been staying at her granny's – you know, old Mr and Mrs Dawkes – or else she'd want to speak to you.'

Poor Joanna, thought Paul. The Dawkes grandparents were very dull and respectable, not in the least like Grandpa, or Paul's own dead grandad.

His own life began to seem not so bad after all, and with Joanna for company things could be very different. The only difficulty would be persuading Megan to have her.

'Well, Paul, what about you? What have you been doing with yourself?'

Paul told her about all the places he had been to, not mentioning that all his exploring had been done on his own. He wanted his aunt to think that Joanna would have just the sort of sight-seeing trips she had in mind, and, besides, it was nice having someone to talk to that long lonely evening. He confided in her his plan to visit all the places on the Monopoly board, which led him on to the game he had played with Ian and the American girl-friend, and that all sounded comfortable and homely to Joanna's mother.

'I'm so glad your mother has time to do all these things with you,' she said. 'I was afraid she might be too busy with her work during the day, and maybe too tired to take you out much at night.'

'Oh, no,' said Paul. 'She's always ready to go out at night.'

'Well, maybe you could ask her to ring me when she gets back. I don't expect she'll be very long, will she? You can mention about Joanna if you like, so that she can think it over before she rings me back. Would there be room for her? Has your mother got enough beds?'

'Oh, yes,' said Paul firmly. He could sleep on the settee in the living-room. He wondered whether to mention about Ian, and decided not to. He hadn't been around since the American girlfriend's visit, anyway. 'But she may be late back tonight. I might have gone to bed.'

'On your own? Does that often happen?'

'Sometimes.'

'Oh. Oh, well, I suppose in a flat it's a bit different. I expect the neighbours keep an eye on you. Are they nice?'

'All right,' said Paul. He'd seen various people in the lift sometimes, whom he assumed lived in the other flats.

Then he heard himself saying something stupid. 'If Joanna can't come, can I come home?'

'What was that, Paul?'

Either the unexpected turn of his thoughts had made her think she had mis-heard him, or she was putting him off, giving herself time to think up excuses. He did not repeat it, but said instead, 'I wondered, if Joanna comes, when she has to go home again.'

'Oh, she'd just stay a few days. We can't ask too much

39

of your poor mother.'

Paul could not help asking, 'Would I come back with her, then?'

'That depends,' said his aunt. She did not say what it depended on, and soon afterwards said goodbye and rang off.

The flat seemed very empty after he had put down the receiver, but the idea that Joanna might come and stay had driven away Paul's dull despair. He picked up the *A – Z* with renewed determination to make sense of it, and found Vine Street in the index. It took a good deal longer to find it on the map, but he did, eventually. Then he had another idea, and got a pen and a piece of paper, and wrote down, in one column, all the places on the Monopoly board he had visited. In another, he put all the other places – it was a much longer column – and settled down with the *A – Z* to find out where they all were.

Megan came home earlier than usual, with Mr Holcombe, to find Paul still poring over the pages of maps.

Mr Holcombe was very friendly, and while Megan was in the kitchen getting something for them to eat, he asked Paul a lot of questions about his life and how long he was staying with his big sister.

'Megan?' said Paul.

'Yes,' said Mr Holcombe. 'She is your sister, isn't she?'

Paul was saved from answering because Megan came in at that moment with a tray of cutlery, which she asked Paul to set out. 'Yes,' she said. 'A bit of an afterthought. There's a big gap between us – people sometimes think he's my son.' She laughed. 'Not very flattering to my age.'

'I could never think that,' said Mr Holcombe. 'How old are you, Paul?'

'Nearly twelve,' said Paul. He laid the table, puzzling. Megan honestly seemed to believe that what she had just said was the truth. At the studio, she had apparently told

40

everyone that Paul was her nephew. Yet to Paul himself, and the rest of the family, she agreed quite happily that she was his mother. Yet now, here she was, without batting an eyelid and without even bothering to make Paul a conspirator beforehand, claiming that he was her little brother. It was as though she did not really know, or care, what was the truth; the only truth was her convenience at the moment of speaking; she would say whatever fitted into the picture she saw herself in at any given time. Just as one day she would appear on a knitting pattern in a thick sweater and a bobble hat, carrying a pair of skis, for all the world as though she were in the Swiss Alps in January, when in fact she was sweating in a stuffy studio in the middle of London in July.

'Ah,' said Mr Holcombe. 'Monopoly. I used to enjoy that when I was your age. Do you get Megan to play with you?'

'No,' said Paul. He explained what he had been doing, and how he had been exploring London while Megan was at work.

'That must cost your sister a pretty penny in bus fares,' said Mr Holcombe. He began to feel inside his breast pocket.

'I've never been on a bus,' said Paul. 'At least, not in London.'

'Never been on a London bus?' exclaimed Mr Holcombe. 'Megan, do you realise you've had your brother here for – how long, Paul? – '

'Thirteen days,' said Paul.

' – and you've never taken him on a London bus?'

'I've been on the Underground,' said Paul. But that was only on the first day, the only day Paul had ever been out in London with Megan.

Megan hesitated as she brought the supper in to them, letting her eyes run over them both as though trying to decide what sort of a person she ought to be this time.

41

'There's nothing I'd like more than to take Paul sight-seeing,' she said, 'but I'm a working woman, Denis, remember?

'There's weekends,' said Mr Holcombe.

'Yes,' said Megan. 'We must try and fit something in this week.' Paul remembered that last Saturday Megan had spent most of the day mooching about the flat in her dressing-gown, irritable because she was waiting for a phone call that didn't come; then Mr Holcombe himself had arrived, with a bunch of roses, and taken her out to dinner, and the next day, Sunday, he had called for her at mid-day and they had been gone all day. Both Megan and Mr Holcombe evidently remembered this, too, and there was an awkward little silence while they did so.

'Tell you what,' said Mr Holcombe. 'Let's all make a day of it sight-seeing next Saturday.'

'I thought . . .' began Megan.

'We can do both,' said Mr Holcombe. 'Paul can amuse himself while we do our little spot of business, and the rest of the time we can go to the Tower, or the Zoo, or whatever you say, Paul.'

'I'd like to go to Liverpool Street station and the Old Kent Road,' said Paul, for his researches had shown him that these were two of the most difficult places to get to on foot.

'Aha,' said Mr Holcombe. 'What about Whitechapel?'

'I haven't discovered where that is,' said Paul.

'All in the same area,' said Mr Holcombe. 'We could combine the lot with a visit to the Tower of London, and H.M.S. *Belfast*.'

'I hope you know what you're taking on,' said Megan.

'Oh, come now; we must give your brother some fun while he's in London, mustn't we? I mean, it isn't as though he's going to be with you for long, is it?' He looked hard at Megan, a forkful of curry halfway to his lips, and she said, 'No, no; it's just to give my sister a bit of a break; she's having a difficult time just now.'

Paul did not look up or stop eating because he sensed that Megan was glancing at him to see if he had reacted to her last remark, but as his jaws continued to chew rhythmically he wondered what she was talking about. What 'difficult time' was Auntie Jean having?

At any rate, this seemed a good moment to bring up another subject that was on his mind. 'Auntie Jean rang,' he said, and paused, wondering how this fitted into the complicated tangle of relationships Megan insisted on weaving, but both she and Mr Holcombe seemed disposed to let it pass. 'She wondered whether Joanna could come and stay here for a few days, and we could do some sight-seeing together.'

'It would be company for you, I suppose,' said Megan, her eyes on Mr Holcombe, waiting for a lead.

'How old is this Joanna, Paul?' asked Mr Holcombe.

'Same age as me,' said Paul. 'Two months younger, actually.'

'Ah,' said Mr Holcombe. 'Pretty?'

'Yes,' said Paul. It was something he had noted from that first day when she came whisking back from ballet class into his grey world. He had never given her any particular credit for the fact, merely noted it, but now he thought, much prettier than Megan with her meaningless plasticine smiles. 'Very,' he said, defiantly. 'She's all right, though,' he added, in case he should have been thought to be condemning her.

His mother had found her line. 'Why, Paul, you are a darling!' she said. 'Of course we must have your Joanna here. She can stay in your room if you don't mind sleeping on the settee, and we'll have a lovely time, showing you both all round London.'

'You're very good to these children, Megan,' said Mr Holcombe. 'Not every career woman would make the time for them.'

'I'm not one of those people who feel a career is every-thing, even in the world of fashion,' said Megan. 'You know that.'

'Yes,' said Mr Holcombe. 'I'm glad.' He put his hand on hers, as though to stop her from getting up, although she had shown no sign of doing so, and said, 'Now, you sit here and have a well-earned rest while Paul and I clear the table.'

Everything went swimmingly. Both Megan and Mr Holcombe seemed to think a lot of Paul that night, and Megan rang her sister and arranged for Joanna to come up and stay over the weekend. She was to arrive on Friday, and accompany them on their visit to the Tower of London – and the Old Kent Road – and stay till Tuesday, which happened to be a day when Mr Dawkes was apparently free from engagements and so could come and spend a day in London with his wife and the children before taking Joanna back with them in the evening.

Before he left, Mr Holcombe's hand found its way again into his breast pocket and this time came out with a wallet, from which he extracted a five pound note. He gave it to Paul. 'For bus fares,' he said.

After he had gone, Megan said, 'Why didn't you ask me for money, Paul? You never said you hadn't got any.'

'I did have some,' said Paul. 'Auntie Jean gave me five pounds, but I've spent most of that on food.'

'But when I've asked you to go to the shops for me, I've always said you can buy something for yourself out of the change, and you never seem to have spent much – you've brought most of it back, so naturally I thought you had plenty of your own.'

'Well, I had,' said Paul, to whom five pounds had seemed a fortune. 'But it's funny where it goes. Ice-creams are terribly expensive in London,' he said sadly.

Megan suddenly laughed, and hugged him. 'I didn't

know you were spending your time going on long-distance hikes,' she said. 'I just thought you were eating at home, out of the larder.'

'I do that too,' said Paul.

It was the end of the day and perhaps her make-up was wearing thin, but Paul noticed, as she looked him up and down, that her face was really quite lined, only with such tiny lines one did not see them at first, and they covered up easily; and that for once there was an expression on her face that seemed to come from inside, rather than as a reflection of the person she was talking to, a look that was part sad, part amused. 'You're just like your father,' she said. 'Fond of your food, and terribly, terribly honest.'

3

Joanna arrived two days later, brought by her Dawkes grandmother on a train that arrived late on Friday afternoon, so that Megan could be there to meet her with Paul; she had evidently grasped that Joanna's grandmother would not be satisfied with a deputy. In fact, it had begun to be plain to Paul that much of the time Megan was 'working' she was not in fact in front of the cameras, but was merely standing about, or sitting drinking endless cups of coffee, waiting for sittings that never materialised, or talking to people who might be able to arrange 'a job' for her. 'Like a dog waiting for crumbs,' Paul had heard Ian remark to his American girlfriend. 'She just won't see she's getting past it.'

'That's not kind,' the girlfriend had said.

'It's just facing facts,' said Ian. 'Which she won't do. Or maybe she is beginning to. I reckon our Denis has turned up just at the right moment.'

All this meant nothing to Paul until he discovered that Mr Holcombe was called Denis. It did not mean a great deal to him even then, because all these people talked about things in such a different way from anything Paul had been accustomed to, but it left him with a stronger impression than before that he did not care much for Ian.

It was good to see Joanna walking demurely up the platform in her scarlet coat beside her neat grey grandmother. She was real in a world of television-screen images of people. For the first few minutes she was untypically silent in the foreign clamour of Paddington station, and it was Paul who appeared more at home. 'How's Prickles?' he said.

'Fine,' said Joanna. 'Only I hardly ever see him. Daddy dotes on him – isn't it funny?'

'How's Grandpa?'

'He's ill,' said Joanna. 'Didn't you know?'

'No. What's the matter with him?'

'I don't know. Pneumonia or bronchitis or something.'

'Since when?'

'Ages,' said Joanna. 'They thought he was going to die, I think. They didn't *say* that, of course, to me, but Mummy kept going to see him, and he's still in hospital. Was all that since you went?'

'He was all right the day I left,' said Paul. 'So far as I know,' he added, anxious not to betray the old man's secret journey.

'That's right,' said Joanna. 'Because when we got back, the Matron rang to say he'd gone off somewhere and they couldn't find him. He didn't turn up till ages after, when someone found him collapsed in the street, somewhere near the station, and took him to hospital.'

'Did he say what he'd been doing?'

'No,' said Joanna. 'He just kept saying it was none of their business. The Matron thinks he can't remember and doesn't want to let on he's getting a bit soft in the nut, but Mummy's not so sure.'

'I'd like to send him a get well card,' said Paul, with memories of all those cards around his grandad's bed when he was taken to hospital. He felt bad about Grandpa, and unforgiving towards Megan, who was meanwhile exchanging polite hostilities with Mrs Dawkes Senior.

All the same, the weekend was a great success. They did all the right tourist things under the kindly guidance of Mr Holcombe, who drove them to the Tower in his car, making a detour to pass Liverpool Street station and Whitechapel. He appeared to enjoy going all over H.M.S. *Belfast* much more than Megan, and insisted that they see everything there was to be seen in the Tower,

47

taking it for granted that Joanna would enjoy the Crown Jewels, which she did, and that Paul would be fascinated by all the armour, which he was, at first, but there was just too much of it and he was quite relieved when Megan reminded Mr Holcombe that they had other things to do after lunch so had better go and get something to eat.

Mr Holcombe was evidently out to impress, because he bought them all the most delicious meal Paul or Joanna had ever eaten, in very grand surroundings. His manner towards Joanna was rather like her father's on one of his best days, and Joanna knew exactly how to charm him; and if she showed off just a shade too much, he did not appear to notice it. But he was also very polite to Megan, making it appear that he thought highly of her for contriving to produce two such delightful children for him to take out, so Megan was happy, too, and lived up to the character he drew for her of being the perfect aunt, or older sister, or whatever she fancied.

Afterwards, they drove over the river, and down the Old Kent Road – Mr Holcombe was certainly good at remembering – and then out through miles of suburbs to the outskirts of London, where the houses were more thinly spaced and the amount of green in the landscape – green trees, green grass – much greater. Paul even saw a field with some cows in it. They came to a smart-looking pub, and drew up in the car park.

'This is where your Auntie Megan and I have some business,' said Mr Holcombe. 'There's a garden round the back where you can play, only don't fall into the river.' He and Megan disappeared into the pub, and Paul and Joanna went willingly enough into the garden, glad to be left to their own devices in the nearest thing to country Paul had seen since he arrived in London.

The garden had a shaggy look. A few round white tables stood, each on a single leg, dotted about the moth-eaten grass, which grew into a straggle round each table

48

leg as though whoever had mowed the lawn, not very lately, could not be bothered to move the tables to do the job properly. Chairs were grouped higgledy-piggledy, probably pushed aside during the same mowing process, and nobody had troubled to set them back round the tables. The flower bed was choked with weeds, and what should have been a trim box hedge shutting the garden off from the car park was full of yawning holes. The smartness, which had caught the eye as they first drew up, was confined to the front. They went to look for the river.

It was there all right, a surprising world of its own slipping quietly away through trailing weeds and hidden behind rising clumps of meadowsweet and loosestrife. A moorhen bobbed among the streamers of pondweed, and a dozen chicks, furry and buoyant as bumble-bees, charted their little ocean; a backwater in the reeds gave them one safe anchorage, a half-submerged pram another.

'Do you suppose,' said Joanna, 'that Mr Holcombe wants to buy this pub?'

'Why should he?' asked Paul, as opaque to new ideas as most boys.

'So that when he marries Auntie Megan, they can run it together.'

'Who said Mr Holcombe is going to marry her?'

'Of course he is. Anyone can see that.'

'Not for sure,' said Paul. Possible, yes; but he was sure Joanna had not taken account of all the other possibilities. She had seen a lot of Mr Holcombe on the one day she had been staying; but if she had been staying longer, she would have seen a lot more people; Ian, for instance. He knew Ian did not want to marry Megan, but it had taken him several days to form this opinion. He could not see how Joanna could be so sure on such thin evidence.

'You'll see,' said Joanna. 'They're probably seeing over the place right now.'

'They're probably in the bar having a drink,' said Paul.

'We'll go and look,' said Joanna, and ran off up the garden. Paul could see her hovering like a humming-bird in flight, on tiptoe on the lawn outside a big window with her arms out to help her keep her balance as she swung her head from side to side, trying to get a clear view inside unblocked by the bright outdoor reflections. Unsuccessful, she tried one or two other windows, but they were either frosted or too high up, so she ran round to the front.

It was the middle of the afternoon, and there was only one other car in the park apart from Mr Holcombe's, and nobody was about. Joanna crouched below the dried-up-looking flowers in the window box and then reared up cautiously. Paul, coming round the corner at a safe distance, saw her and turned to study the car, blushing for her in case someone should come by.

'There's no one in the bar,' she said, and walked in at the open door. Paul kept a safe distance, but moved so that he had a view down the corridor. Suddenly there were voices, friendly if a little surprised, and he heard Joanna saying politely, 'Sorry to bother you, but Paul wanted to know where the toilet was.' A few moments later she re-emerged, and beckoned to him. 'It's here,' she said, aloud. 'I'll show you the way.'

Paul had to submit as the victim of this piece of cunning with as good a grace as he could muster, muttering, 'Why me? Why not you?'

'I was right,' whispered Joanna. 'I'll tell you later.'

She had achieved more than information, however, for when Paul rejoined her in the garden she was sitting at one of the tables with two tall glasses of Coke and two packets of peanuts.

'Did Mr Holcombe buy these?' said Paul.

'No,' said Joanna. 'The man gave us them; and he was giving them drinks, too.'

'He'd have to,' said Paul. 'It's not opening time.' Long years accompanying farmers on market days had made Paul familiar with such things. 'They wouldn't be allowed to buy them.'

'Why did they come, then?' said Joanna. 'Anyway, they were in the kitchen, looking at the stoves. Mr Holcombe was saying, "What do you think, darling?" or something like that.'

Paul was silenced. He drank his Coke through the straw, slowly, to make it last. He felt fretful and irritated but did not know why.

'Will you come and live here with them?' said Joanna, and her cheerful leap into an unknown future showed Paul the root of his own discontent.

'I don't know,' he said. Then he repeated it, in anger. 'I don't know. Don't you see? That's what it's always like for me. It's all very well for you to plan for Mr Holcombe to marry Megan, and to buy this pub and all that; it's just a game to you.'

Joanna did not entirely understand, though she tried to. 'I'd have thought that would be quite fun,' she said. 'I mean, always to know what's going to happen, same old home, same old school, same old clothes, same old ballet classes, same old friends – it can get awfully *boring*.'

'I suppose so,' said Paul, not really listening. 'But you say, shall I come and live at this pub and all that? Well, supposing Mr Holcombe *does* marry Megan, supposing they *do* buy this pub, how do I know they'll have me here? Even if I do want to?'

'Do you want to?'

'What's the use of my wanting anything? Supposing I don't? Maybe I could live with you – but only if your parents want me. I don't want to live with people who don't want to have me, don't you see? And I can't see that anybody wants to have me, not really wants. I don't belong anywhere any more. You do. Don't you see?'

51

Joanna cast about in her mind for something to say, and found the wrong thing. 'They'd be more likely to want you if you didn't do stupid things like running away.'

'I know,' said Paul. 'That's just it.' It was too true to be worth getting angry about. 'That's what I mean. If *you* did something like that, they might be very angry, but you'd still belong. But when I do, they say, "Why worry? He doesn't really belong here. We'll get rid of him." '

Joanna wanted to unravel some of what she had said. 'You do belong,' she said. 'You belong to me.'

'Thanks,' said Paul. 'How much did you pay for me?'

'You are the only cousin I've got, and I've got no brothers or sisters, so that makes having a cousin quite special. I'm the only cousin you've got, too.' She bent down and detected a small smile on Paul's face. 'That's something, isn't it?'

'Yes,' said Paul. 'That's something. But I wish I'd got a proper mother and father like you, even if. . . .'

'If what?'

'Never mind.' This was not the moment to be grudging about Uncle William.

'You've got a mother.'

'I said a proper one. Megan keeps pretending she's my sister half the time. Or my aunt.'

'Whatever for?'

'I think she told them at work I was her nephew because she wants to seem younger than she is; they want young women for these advertisements and such. Have you ever seen a middle-aged woman in an advertisement?'

'No.'

'And she wants Mr Holcombe to think I'm her brother.'

'That's barmy. He's much older than her anyway. Do you suppose she doesn't want him to think she's already married?'

'He knows she was; she told him once about how she

was left a young widow when her husband died and she had to take up this modelling to earn her living.'

'But that's not true, exactly, is it?'

'No. I'll tell you what I think, but it only makes sense if you're right about her wanting to marry him.'

'Of course I'm right. It's obvious.'

'She doesn't really want me for keeps. If she told Mr Holcombe I was her son when they got married, he'd expect her to have me, wouldn't he?'

'But why shouldn't she want you for keeps?'

Paul was twiddling his straw into a circlet, but there wasn't enough of it, so he put out his hand and took Joanna's from her glass and began to weave it in, 'I don't think she wants anything for keeps,' he said. 'Not Grandpa, not my father, not her job, not me.'

'Not Mr Holcombe? He's nice. I like him.'

'I wouldn't know about Mr Holcombe,' said Paul. He was not so quick with his likes and dislikes as Joanna. 'Of course,' he added, 'it could be she thinks Mr Holcombe won't marry her if he thinks he's got to take me along as well.' He looked across at Joanna gazing at him mournfully, and grinned. He felt better for having worked all that out, and grateful to Joanna for being there to share it with him. 'Here you are,' he said. 'A ring for a very special cousin,' and he handed her the straw circle.

'A ring!' said Joanna. It was about two inches across. 'What do you think I am? An elephant?'

'Well, whatever you call those things you put round your wrist.'

'A bracelet,' said Joanna, already slipping it over her thin hand. 'Thank you, Paul. It is beautiful. At least, it would be if it wasn't so sticky and didn't smell of Coke.' She was up and away, pirouetting around the lawn, waving her arms above her head to show off the bracelet.

'Chuck it away then,' said Paul, who was a realist.

53

'Never!' said Joanna. 'I shall keep it till my dying day. We'll wash it in the river.'

Ten minutes later two dripping figures knocked at the pub door.

'I fell in the river,' said Joanna. 'And Paul fell in getting me out.'

4

The next day Megan took them to the Zoo, where they met Mr Holcombe outside the entrance. They were told to be back there in three hours' time, and that was all they saw of Megan or Mr Holcombe until the end of the day. 'Perhaps,' said Paul, 'he doesn't like getting his car all wet.'

'The Zoo is quite a dry place,' said Joanna, but then they found the penguins and the sea-lions.

'If you fall in there,' said Paul, 'don't do it at three o'clock.'

'Why not?'

Paul pointed to the notice. *Feeding time 3 o'clock*, it said.

They had fun at the Zoo, though Paul had a few sad moments when they came upon an enclosure full of goats, for they reminded him of his pet goat, Davy. He found Joanna was an expensive person to have around, not only because she could not resist buying sweets and ices all the time but also the special bags of food for the various animals. She spent all the two pounds her mother had given her, but Paul would not spend more than one pound fifty of Mr Holcombe's present, because there was still tomorrow to live through with Joanna on his hands, and he was pretty sure that once Mr Holcombe was back at his job – whatever that was – Megan would also disappear to hers, leaving Paul to entertain his cousin.

That evening, when they got back to Megan's flat, accompanied by Mr Holcombe this time, Mr Holcombe said, 'Megan and I have got something to tell you.'

'I told you,' said Joanna to Paul.

'What did you tell him?' asked Mr Holcombe, but Joanna lost her nerve and would not go on. Only when

Mr Holcombe had announced, with due solemnity, that he and Megan intended to get married, Joanna said triumphantly, 'That's what I told him.'

'You are a perspicacious little baggage,' said Mr Holcombe, delighted. 'And what did you think, young man?'

Paul did not feel that this was the right moment to express some of the things he had thought, so contented himself with asking, 'Are you going to buy that pub we went to yesterday?'

'Thinking about it,' said Mr Holcombe. 'There speaks the man of business. Yes, we're thinking about it, aren't we, Megan? It's what every city man dreams of: to get a beautiful wife and settle down and run a pub in the country together.'

For Joanna, Megan's job was still full of romance. 'Won't it be rather dull,' she said, 'washing glasses and laying tables instead of being a top fashion model?'

Megan laughed; she liked the word 'top'. 'One can't go on doing that sort of thing for ever,' she said.

'We'll employ staff to do the washing-up and lay the tables,' said Mr Holcombe. 'Of course, that place has run down a lot in recent years, but it could be a money-spinner, a real money-spinner. Just think what one could do with that riverside garden, for a start. And we'll expand the restaurant side of it – maybe the odd cabaret; I see it becoming a popular resort for rich businessmen to come for an evening out of town. All sorts of possibilities.' He looked down benignly at Paul and Joanna. 'But the main thing is I've managed to persuade your Aunt Megan to go into it with me, and with her gifts and support there's no knowing what we shall achieve.'

'What about Paul?' said Joanna.

In the short silence that followed, Paul turned brick red. Silly fool, Joanna.

'What *about* Paul?' said Mr Holcombe.

'I expect she means can he come and stay sometimes, at the hotel, is that it?' asked Megan.

'Yes,' said Joanna. 'That's what I meant.'

'Well, of course, both of you, when we're not too busy, in the off-season. Welcome any time – so long as you don't fall in the river.' Mr Holcombe laughed merrily, and then said it was time Megan got ready, as he was taking her out to dinner for a little celebration.

'Who's looking after us?' said Joanna.

'You'll be all right,' said Megan. 'There's people in the flat next door. You don't want me to leave anything for you, do you? I mean, you'd rather forage for yourselves, I expect.'

'Have a good fry-up,' said Mr Holcombe.

After they had gone, Joanna said, 'Do they often do this? Go out and leave you to get your own supper?'

'Pretty often.'

'How odd. Don't you get lonely, here on your own?'

'There's the telly. And I like getting my own supper. What shall we have?'

'Can you cook, Paul?'

'I often used to cook supper when I was with Grandad. Eggs and bacon and stuff like that.'

'I can make sponge cakes,' said Joanna. 'And pepper-mint creams. And fruit tarts.' Cooking for Joanna was a kind of afternoon's treat when her mother was on hand to help her, not a means of getting fed.

'Can you make syrup tart? I like that.'

'I don't see why not,' said Joanna, on her mettle.

They had a delicious meal. Paul fried up about everything friable he could find, and if Joanna's syrup tart was like no other syrup tart either of them had eaten before, it made excellent toffee, and relieved Paul of the last of his baby teeth, which had been tiresomely wobbly of late. Joanna told him he must put it under his pillow and get his fairy fivepence.

'Who do you suppose will put it there?' said Paul.

'The fairies,' said Joanna, fatuously.

'Don't be daft. Who puts your fairy fivepence under your pillow?'

'Mummy, I suppose. Or Daddy.'

'Yeah, well, I may as well put my tooth in the rubbish bin.' He went to lift the lid.

'No, don't do that. I will. Go on, put it under your pillow.'

'You haven't got it. You spent all your money at the Zoo.'

'I'll find something.' She took the tooth from his hand, looked at it, said 'Ugh,' and put it under the cushion on the settee. 'That's where you sleep,' she said. 'Don't forget to look in the morning.'

'Jo,' said Paul. 'Megan said something to Mr Holcombe about Auntie Jean being in some sort of trouble. What did she mean?'

'She said that?'

'Something of the sort. She said —' Paul thought, trying to remember the exact words — 'her sister was having a difficult time just now. Is she?'

'Not that I know of. Perhaps she meant because Grandpa was ill.'

'But she was explaining why I was staying here, and he wasn't ill till after I came. Anyway,' he added, crossly, 'that ought to be her trouble, too. He's her father as well, though you mightn't think it for all she cares. Why were you staying with your grandparents? And why aren't you going to Spain after all?'

'I was staying with them because of Mummy spending so much time with Grandpa, and Daddy being so busy just now. And it was something to do with Daddy's work that we couldn't go to Spain. It's terribly boring at the grandparents.'

'I bet.' Paul wondered whether to tell Joanna about seeing Uncle William and Auntie Jean through the window the night he couldn't sleep, but decided not to. She was so quick to notice things and to jump to conclusions, that if there was anything wrong at home she would surely have noticed, and just as surely have told him. She was not good at holding things back; Paul did not suppose she had ever tried.

She had tried; she had been trying for some time not to tell Paul something that was in her mind, but it was nothing to do with home, and anyway at that moment she lost the battle, lost it out of her longing to help Paul. She felt for him tonight, because of the tooth and because of what Mr Holcombe had said about him maybe staying at the pub in the off-season, when they were not too busy, more than she had felt for him yesterday in the garden. Now she was beginning to understand better what it meant not to belong.

'Supposing,' she said, 'supposing your father isn't dead after all, and the police manage to find him, just like they found your mother; wouldn't that be exciting?'

'That's a silly thing to suppose. He is dead.'

'Are you sure? How do you know?'

'Grandad said he was dead.'

'What did he die of? Was there a funeral?'

'I don't know.'

'But you would know, wouldn't you? I mean, when people die, all the family go to the funeral. You'd remember. After all, you can remember your father, can't you?'

'Only just.' He remembered the hands, helping him hold the bottle for the lamb, and a face with round brown eyes and floppy hair. It might not have been his father; it could have been someone else, but it had always stuck in his mind that it was his father, and he had clung to the notion until it had grown to be taken for granted. 'Anyway, why are you on about it?'

'Because. . . .' Now Joanna hesitated, but she saw she

59

had gone too far to draw back. 'Well, Mummy told me that he just sort of disappeared, and no one really knew what happened to him.'

'Went off, you mean, like Megan? He wouldn't have done that.'

'No, not exactly. He went away to find work, and came home when he could to see you.'

'That's when I remember him.'

'Well, Mummy said he suddenly stopped coming, and didn't write or anything, and didn't come to the funeral when your grandmother died, so they thought he must be dead. But he could just have been very ill, or lost his memory, or emigrated to Australia and not had enough money to come back; lots of things.'

Paul looked at her and thought how all that made sense. He wondered why he had never asked his grandad for the answers to questions such as these and it made him see how not just everything had changed for him when Grandad died, but how he himself had changed. That boy with the cropped hair and old-fashioned trousers plodding up the hill with the cans of paraffin and Aunty Mary's cakes, that boy, who took life as it came and never asked questions, that boy was as dead as his grandfather, as dead as Davy. Where had he gone to? And who was this boy, Paul, now?

'I wish you hadn't said that,' he said.

'I'm sorry. I thought it might cheer you up, to think there might be a real father, looking for you, who might suddenly turn up one day.'

'If he was looking for me, he'd know where to find me,' said Paul. 'At the farm.'

'But you're not there now.'

'Mr Abraham is, and all the neighbours. My father grew up there, don't forget; he could soon find out where I'd gone if he tried. And he would try. So he must be dead.'

'Mr Abraham came to see us the other day,' said Joanna.

'*Mr Abraham*? Whatever for?'

'Something to do with buying the farm, I think.'

'You never said.'

'I forgot.'

'You can't forget *Mr Abraham*.'

'I didn't forget *him*. I forgot to tell you. He's funny, isn't he?'

'I like him.'

'I liked him, too, but I didn't see much of him. He scarcely spoke to me.' Joanna yawned. 'I'm tired,' she said. 'When will they come back?'

'Not for ages, probably. We don't need to wait up for them.'

'Seems funny, going to bed with no grown-ups in the house.'

'You'd get used to it if you stayed here long. Anyway,' he added, for it seemed to be the magic formula, 'there's people in the flat next door.'

'Do you know them?'

'No.' Paul was more than ready for bed. The mention of Mr Abraham had given his thoughts a happier turn. He wanted to sleep while he could remember the feel of being a giant on the roof, looking for UFOs, and not a boy who did not belong to anybody. 'I'm going to bed anyhow, and as I go to bed here and will be putting the light out, you'd better go too.'

Joanna went off to get undressed, but when Paul came back from the bathroom she was in the living-room again. 'Do you mind if I leave my door open?' she said. Her room opened off the living-room. 'It feels spooky without anyone in the flat.'

'Do as you like.' Paul snuggled down on the sofa, feeling warm and cosy. Mr Abraham was right; the world was an exciting place, it was just a matter of looking at

61

it the right way. It had been fun exploring London on his own and, in a different way, these last two days when he had company. Tomorrow would be different again; just him and Joanna, looking for Monopoly places. He would take her on the Underground, perhaps even on a bus. He still had three pounds fifty. Then the next day Auntie Jean would be coming up, and and Uncle William; he even felt quite warm at the thought of seeing Uncle William again. After all, Uncle William did like Prickles, and he had tried to be kind, in his way.

He remembered his tooth; if he had lost it at Joanna's home, instead of here, Auntie Jean would have put some money under his pillow; if she usually did that for Joanna, he was sure of it. He put his hand up under the cushion to find it; instead, he found a coin – no, a button.

He brought it out and squinted at it in the light that slanted in from the street. He knew what it was: it was a coin that had been made into a button, a foreign silver coin with strange markings on it. It was Joanna's lucky button. That's what she always called it – her lucky button. She had found it years ago on the beach, long before she met Paul, and always kept it in her coat pocket. Paul remembered the fuss she had made once when she thought she had lost it. Now she had given it to Paul, in exchange for his tooth, because she had spent all her money.

'Joanna,' he called softly, but there was no answer. Soon he was sleeping too, the button still safe in his hand.

The next day, the day of their private exploration, started well. Joanna was delighted with the Park, and Park Lane and Marble Arch and Oxford Street and Bond Street and Regent Street, where Paul took her in pursuit of Monopoly places. But when, eventually, they arrived at Piccadilly Circus, Joanna was flagging, so they found an ice-cream shop like the one Paul had discovered on the first day, and that revived them enough to plod on to Trafalgar Square. A lot of people seemed to be sitting about in Trafalgar Square, many of them eating, which seemed an excellent idea. Not far away there was a shop selling hot dogs and sandwiches and fizzy drinks, and they sat in the sun among the pigeons and lions for a long time, eating and resting. Paul was busy with his Monopoly list and the *A – Z*, working out how to get to places like Vine Street and the Angel, Islington, but Joanna said it was all very well, he had other days in which to do his thing, and what she would really like to do was see Buckingham Palace and ride on a bus and the escalator and the deepest Underground there was.

Paul disappeared into his reference book again, while Joanna watched the pigeons and the passers-by, and cricked her neck gazing up at Nelson on his column. At last Paul announced that they would have to walk to Buckingham Palace, and if she wanted to travel on the Underground they might as well go on to St James's Park and take the Underground to the Angel, Islington. 'And from there,' he said, excitedly, 'it looks as if we could get a bus that would take us down Pentonville Road – that's one of the places – and Euston Road – oh, great, that's all the pale blues – we'd pass some of the stations, too, and end up near Megan's flat.' One of Paul's worries about taking a bus, though he didn't admit it to Joanna, was that he might not know when to get off; he preferred to venture into the unknown on the Underground, where all the stations were clearly marked, and use the bus to get him back to home ground, with which, from his previous journeys and a good many shopping trips done for Megan, he was pretty familiar. What he failed to take into account was that buses, unlike the Underground, did not necessarily follow what looked like the most obvious routes on the

63

map, but were guided by the unseen movements of people from one part of London to another, and subject to such hazards as one-way streets. He saw a broad highway marked on his map running more or less direct from the Angel to the Edgware Road, which he knew already; it looked foolproof.

By the time they had inspected Buckingham Palace and found St James's, they were both ready enough to sink into the dusty seats for what Joanna hoped would be a long long journey. All the same, she was nervous about plunging into the station, getting tickets, following arrows and negotiating those echoing tunnels without an overseeing adult, and admired Paul's unhurried care and coolness in getting them to the right platform. When their train drew into the next station, and they saw it was, indeed, the one they had hoped it would be, they exchanged glances of self-congratulation. It was only after they had sat in the swaying train for quite a time checking the stations off on the plan above their heads, that Paul said, 'Actually, we may have to get off at King's Cross, and walk back to the Angel.'

'Why?' said Joanna. 'Are we on the wrong train?'

'We might not be,' said Paul cautiously. 'But they split up and go in different directions, I think.' He was right; their train suddenly went off at a tangent and the next station proved to be Aldgate East, which was quite off their route. They had to bundle out in a hurry and once more study the direction signs and negotiate the maze of tunnels. Joanna's faith in Paul was beginning to wane, and her stamina to fail; besides, the place was gloomy and almost unused at this time of day, before the afternoon rush hour; the few people who stood about on the platforms looked sinister and unfriendly, and no cheerful bearded guitarists enlivened the tunnels as they had done on the stations they had been at with Megan the previous day.

'Come on,' said Paul, as a train caterpillared in to their chosen platform. 'I think this is right.'

'Oh, Paul, are you sure?'

'I said I *think*,' said Paul a little crossly, for the responsibility was beginning to weigh on him now things were not going quite so smoothly.

To his relief, all was well, and they were soon pulling into King's Cross, but the magic of exploring had somehow gone. King's Cross was not a simple place like St James's, and when they finally plunged out into the sunlight after long wanderings and an infinity of turns, they had not the slightest idea where they stood.

'Is it a long way to the Angel, Paul?' asked Joanna plaintively, while Paul tried vainly to find some relation between the map in his hand and the section of London that confronted him.

'Are you lost? Can I help you at all?' said a deep voice in Joanna's ear, and she turned round, startled, to see a large man, with a thick black beard and bright eyes, his face close to her own. She was very tired, and getting increasingly nervous about being in a strange part of London. She gave a yelp of fright and ran off down the road, dragging Paul after her.

The man took a few steps after them, his hands held out in a reassuring gesture. 'It's all right,' he said. 'I will not eat you.'

Paul turned, still towed backwards by Joanna, who held his hand in a fevered clutch. 'Thank you,' he shouted. 'We're not lost.' But other people had come between them, and Paul was not sure whether he heard. The man turned and crossed the road onto an island, and was obviously making his way peacefully about his business, but he had the kindness to turn and look back at them, catching Paul's bothered look. He waved and gave a friendly and forgiving grin before disappearing into the stream of traffic.

'Now you've got me all muddled,' Paul snapped.

'You're no more muddled than you were before,' said Joanna swiftly. 'Anyway, you *know* you shouldn't talk to strangers.'

'If you scream and run away every time you see a stranger in London, you'd have a busy time,' said Paul.

'I *didn't* scream.'

'You did.'

They bickered as they walked, hoping eventually to come upon some street name that they could fit onto the map. But then Paul suddenly saw a bus labelled *Euston*. 'Quick!' he said. 'That's what we want.' It was actually at traffic lights, and moved off just as they scrambled on, bringing the wrath of the conductor down on their heads. When he came round for their fares, and Paul said, guessing, 'Edgware Road, please,' he made some remark they could not hear, took their money and passed on. 'What did you say?' said Paul, but the conductor had gone whistling upstairs.

Some time later he returned, and worked his way up the aisle again, while Paul was staring anxiously out of the window looking for familiar landmarks. After he had passed, he glanced back at them and said, 'Hey, you still here? You didn't pay to come this far. Where you getting off, then?'

'Edgware Road,' said Paul.

'Which part?'

Paul didn't really know which part; any bit that he recognised would do. He mentioned the only name he could remember. 'By Marble Arch,' he said.

'You've come on the wrong bus for that, sonny,' said the conductor. 'We're nearly in Kilburn now.' He looked at their anxious faces and became quite kind. 'Tell you what,' he said. 'If you get off at the next stop, it's only a short walk to where you can get a bus that takes you right to Marble Arch. You can't miss it; it says Marble Arch up on the front.' He gave them directions, to which Paul tried to listen intelligently, but they were at the stop before he had got it clear in his mind.

'This is it,' said the conductor. He bent down to point down a side street. 'Down there,' he said. 'First right; keep on to the traffic lights, then left, and right again at the second traffic lights after that. You'll see the bus stop just down the road from there.'

The bus gathered speed and moved off, leaving them in one of those areas that all large cities have, where every street looks exactly the same. By the time they reached the first set of traffic lights they had forgotten which way to turn off.

For the next half hour they wandered disconsolately, looking for bus stops; twice they summoned up courage to ask passers-by but in both cases they were strangers.

'I thought you *knew* London,' said Joanna, too tired to be fair. As always on these occasions, it felt as though they had walked miles and were doomed to go on walking for the rest of their lives. The streets were beginning to fill up with people and traffic, for the rush hour was approaching. Paul began to panic because he had seen how in the rush hour long queues hustled at the bus stops, and the Undergrounds swarmed with uncaring people like bees. The sight of that hurly-burly was one of the reasons why hitherto he had fought shy of using public transport, preferring the security of his own legs. But now he had no means of knowing how to find his way home on foot, and suspected it was much too far. He tried to make sense of his little book, but it was difficult to follow at the best of times, when his mind was clear and he had some recognisable touchstone, like Hyde Park or Nelson's Column; here there was nothing, and he was too befuddled to unravel it.

'We could ask a policeman,' he said, admitting defeat, but there were no policemen to be seen. At the next corner they did, however, see some traffic lights a couple of hundred metres down the road on their right, so they began to walk towards them.

'Look!' cried Joanna. 'A bus!' It was approaching the lights from the far side, and halted as they changed to amber, and then red, but the left-hand indicator was flashing, so they knew that as soon as the green lit up, the bus would swing off in that direction.

'Quick!' said Paul. 'Run!' He charged down the road, but Joanna was faster. She was ahead of him as she raced across the entrance to a side street, her whole mind fixed on the bus, still winking at the cross-roads.

'Stop!' yelled Paul, for he saw the van; Joanna wavered, and in that instant crumpled like a shattered bird.

For a timeless moment, the scene cut into Paul's brain in total, unreal silence; the look of sudden terror on the face turned back to him, the upflung arms, the dirty white van lurching forward a little on its springs after the wheels had skidded to a halt. Then the noises of the real world caught up with him: the squeal of tyres, which must have sounded earlier, but his brain had not registered it, the cries of women, the street suddenly full of running feet and bodies coming between the unimportant boy and the scene of the accident; and a man with a drooping moustache bursting out of the van like a wild creature and shouting, 'Bloody, bloody, *bloody* kid.' Nobody else paid the man any attention, for they were crowding round the child on the road but the violence of him was the only thing at that moment that focused Paul's shocked attention. The man glanced in front of the van and walked quickly away, straight towards Paul. Perhaps because Paul was the only person looking at him, he spoke to him.

'She ran straight out; Christ, she came from nowhere; bloody kid, came from nowhere.' Now he wasn't shouting, scarcely more than whispering; he gripped Paul's

68

shoulder with a hand that shook. He wasn't speaking to Paul as though he were a child. He wanted something from Paul that Paul could not give, and Paul was frightened. He backed away, scared of the white sweaty face and the quivering grip; the man turned from him and rested his hand, instead, upon the brick wall; suddenly he crouched low and vomited on the pavement.

Reality dropped back onto Paul, and the fog of shock began to clear. He walked firmly forward, shouldering his way through the small crowd, and looked down on Joanna. She lay spreadeagled on her back, one leg horribly angled. Her coat, scarlet as blood against the grey pavement, had a great dirty smear right across it; some small corner of Paul's brain noted this, and knew she would not like her coat to be dirty like that. Dark lashes curved below the closed lids against a pale, smudged face; the narrow wrist that stuck out of the coat sleeve was braceleted with the circlet of drinking straws. Slowly he put his hand into his pocket and felt with his fingers for Joanna's lucky button, the one she would never be parted from, until she had given it to him for his lost tooth.

He knelt beside her and thrust the button into her hand, closing the nerveless fingers round the little lump of metal. Somebody said, 'Keep away,' and another voice, more gently, said, 'It's best not to move her, lovey; there's a doctor just coming.' The limp fingers would not hold the button, so he put it carefully into her coat pocket. Then he looked up at the ring of strange faces.

'She's my cousin,' he said. 'She belongs to me.'

5

'Concussion,' said the ambulance man, for it was he, and not a doctor, who arrived with wailing siren a few moments later. 'And a fractured leg. Easy, now.' He and his mate slid her smoothly onto a stretcher. 'Who's with her?' His eyes glanced round the nearer faces, to see who had a claim to be allowed into the ambulance.

'I am,' said Paul.

The man's gaze dropped to Paul's level, where he still crouched on the pavement. 'Only you?' he said. 'Not got no grown-up with you?'

'No,' said Paul. He kept his hand on the stretcher rail as they lifted it, suddenly afraid that Joanna would disappear into the ambulance, the doors close and the vehicle drive off into the unknown, leaving him standing on the pavement.

'Does your mum live close by?' asked the man. 'Close enough for you to nip along and tell her what's happened?'

'No,' said Paul. He wanted to get into that ambulance quick, and no more questions, so that Joanna should not be stuck here in the street, the cold unseeing centre of so many curious eyes, and he gave the simplest answer that came to mind. 'She lives in Wales; we're just staying in London, with an auntie.'

The stretcher was slotted in now. 'Hop in, then,' the man said. 'You can tell me how to get in touch with your auntie as we go.' As the man got up behind him and began to pull the doors to, Paul glimpsed a policeman moving around the crowd, with his notebook open. He remembered the white-faced driver being sick on the pavement. 'I ought to tell the policeman,' he said. He felt bad about the driver, as though he had failed him in some way when he clutched at him with shaking hands. He felt he should make amends. 'It wasn't the driver's fault,' he said.

'It never is,' said the ambulance man, absently. He was holding Joanna's wrist and listening. 'The police will come round and ask questions later, very like. If you give me your address now, in London that is, we can get on to your auntie right away, soon as we reach the hospital.'

Paul gave it. 'But she'll still be at work, probably,' he said.

'Where's that, then?'

'I don't know. She goes to different places.' He started to try and explain, but the man had lost interest. It did not seem very important to Paul, either, so he fell into silence, staring at Joanna's still form.

'Home address?' said the man, but he had to repeat it before Paul realised he was waiting to take it down. He gave it, and asked, 'Is she going to be all right?'

'Just a moment. Telephone number?'

'Pardon?'

'Are your parents on the phone?'

'Oh – oh, yes.'

'Number?'

Paul stared at him, distressed. It was gone. All this time he had remembered that number, like a lifeline; now, it was gone. He had got it written down, but it was in his suitcase under Joanna's bed. 'I – I can't remember,' he said. His eyes rested on the stretcher. 'She knows it,' he said.

He glanced at the man, and quickly back to Joanna, afraid to let him see the question in his thoughts, yet wanting the answer. Would the ambulance man say, 'That's all right then; she'll tell us in a few minutes, when she comes round?' Or was it no use that Joanna knew the telephone number, no use now or ever again?

'I'm sorry,' he said. 'I do know it, only it's gone. I sort

71

of know it. I've got it written down at – at my auntie's.'

'Don't worry,' said the man. 'Directory enquiries will tell us, soon enough. We're turning into the hospital now.'

Paul felt as though he were a small creature that had unexpectedly been swallowed whole by an enormous monster. Half an hour ago, he and Joanna were in sole charge of themselves, trying to organise their lives, not very successfully, in a world that seemed totally ignorant of their existence. Now they had become the centre of attention of a great network of organisations – the ambulance service, the police force, the huge hospital buildings which he could see encircling him on every side, even the post office. By running under the van, Joanna had brought them to the attention of a computer programmer; Paul had given the magic formula – his name and address – and now they were whirling help-lessly through the ticking machine. It made him feel less important, not more; he had lost a part of himself, but did not know what it was.

One thing he knew, and so he held tightly to the stretcher rail as the men slid Joanna out and onto the wheeled trolley for the next stage through the computer: he must not let the machine split them off into two separate units. If he did, they might get whirled apart, spinning through different electronic circuits, never to be reunited. The link with Joanna was the only thing left that made him feel like a person, especially now that the kindly ambulance man had disappeared, his place taken by equally kindly white-coated porters. They in turn were replaced by other men in white coats, by a woman, not in uniform, with grey hair, by nurses in various kinds of hats and with various coloured hands and faces.

Eventually the inevitable occurred, and Paul found himself sitting on an orange-coloured stacking chair in a place labelled *Casualty Waiting Room*. The room was partly full of healthy-looking people who talked and joked and knitted and helped themselves to cups of hot drinks from a vending machine in the corner. A small child nagged unceasingly for twenty pence for the slot machine next door, selling chocolate bars. 'You're being silly,' said the mother. 'It only sells fruit-and-nut, and you know you don't like that.' But in the end she gave in, and the child came back, unwrapping the bar. 'I don't like it,' he said, after the first bite. 'Can I have money for a drink, Mum?'

Paul became increasingly afraid that Joanna had been taken away and nobody had remembered about him. Once, he summoned up enough courage to go to the counter marked *Enquiries* where there was a woman in a green uniform. 'Don't worry, dear; they'll tell you when there's anything to tell.' She made no effort to pick up one of the telephones or go and knock on any of the private-looking doors across the corridor, but as Paul turned to go, a machine buzzed on her desk, and he paused, hopefully. 'Mrs Watson to Room Number Five', said the woman into a speaker that made her voice come out of a box high up on the wall, and the mother with the nagging child got up and left the waiting room. Paul went and sat down again, staring at his shoes for what seemed like hours. It reminded him of the time he had waited for his mother at the top of the stairs, his first day in London, alone among strangers.

Yet he hoped that his mother would not come, because he was afraid that if she did, the hospital authorities would expect her to stay, waiting for Joanna to regain consciousness, and he would be sent home, because he was only eleven. That was wrong, wrong for his mother, who would be bored, wrong for Joanna who cared nothing for her Auntie Megan, and wrong for him. Age had nothing to do with some things. He was older than his mother. She would go to the vending machine and buy a cup of tea, and come back making a face and saying it was horrible. She had wanted his father, and then left him. She wanted lots of things, but . . . Paul dismissed her from his mind. Mr Holcombe could have her.

He wondered about his father, and what Joanna had said – was it only last night? Could it be true that he was alive? His mind came back to Joanna. It kept doing that, going round in a circle of other thoughts that always brought him back again to Joanna, lying unconscious and broken, and the question: Was she going to die?

He knew it could happen. Grandad had died, and Nana; his father, too, probably; and Davy was dead. He had none of the confidence so many people feel that it could not happen to their family. He knew it could, because it had happened before.

But he could not anchor his mind to this single point, although he tried. This was what he was here for; he felt as though it was a betrayal to be thinking of anything else except this one thing. He tried to tie his mind to the present need with a string of words. *Please God, let her get better*. That way, it was a prayer; it made him feel he was doing good. But while the top of his mind repeated the words over and over again, underneath the current of his thoughts had gone eddying away again on another spin round the whirlpool. *Was* his father alive? Supposing he walked in, now, suddenly, to take charge? He would not be a little man like Uncle William, or Mr Holcombe, or Ian, silly little men with silly little ways, and he would not be old, like Grandad and Grandpa and Mr Abraham. He would come in now, and smooth away all this worry and anxiety at the hospital, and take Paul away to live with him, and he would know all the right things to do, and all the answers. He would be a friend and a father, and everything would be all right again. Even his goat, Davy, would be alive again. . . .

74

That thought tripped him up like an unseen doorstep, and he stumbled over it into bitter reality.

Nobody could bring Davy back, and his father was a vague figure with round brown eyes and floppy hair who had gone to pieces when Megan had left him, let down his old parents and lost touch with his son. The picture would not fit, try as Paul might to drag the pieces together into the shape of a hero. Only if he were dead could he be a hero.

Dead. His mind had gone full circle again. *Please, God, make her better. . . .* However much longer would he have to wait?

He looked up, and there was Mr Abraham standing in front of him.

Whatever was he doing here? Paul just stared at him, too dazed to say anything.

'They've just brought Joanna out,' said Mr Abraham. 'They're taking her up to the ward now. Come along, we'll go with her.' He led Paul out into the corridor and smartly into the same lift as the trolley being wheeled ahead of them by two orderlies, before the doors had time to close. Joanna lay on the trolley, looking exactly the same, pale and unconscious.

'Relative?' enquired one of the orderlies.

'Yes,' said Mr Abraham. The doors sighed shut and the lift rose up through the heart of the huge hospital. Paul laid his hand on the side of the trolley, as though to repair the broken link, and spoke, for the first time, to Mr Abraham. 'Why are you here?' he said. The sense of being no more than a punched card flying through an electronic maze melted away. He was a human being again, with a friend; very much a human, for Mr Abraham did not seem the kind of person who would agree to be slotted into a system. The way he had coolly walked into the lift proved that.

'Chance,' said Mr Abraham. 'Or Providence. I wanted

75

to see you about something, so I came round to your mother's flat to look for you. I was ringing the door bell when the policeman arrived to tell your mother about the accident.'

'She wasn't at home, was she?'

'No, so I thought I'd come along myself.'

'I'm glad.' Paul could not say any more, for relief flooded through him in a wave that nearly choked him, but he deliberately looked up at his friend to let those inquisitive old eyes read his face. People usually had to guess at Paul's feelings from the back of his neck.

Mr Abraham stared at him, making no attempt to hide his own concern behind a mask of jollity. 'How bad are things?' he asked. The lift was stopping.

'I don't know,' said Paul. 'Can't you ask them?' He glanced at the orderlies now wheeling the trolley out again.

'They won't know,' said Mr Abraham. 'But we'll find somebody up at the ward who does, I expect.'

He did. Although Paul had to be left once more sitting in a corridor, he was no longer afraid that he was going to be forgotten, or lost, or sent away. In a little while Mr Abraham came back to him, carrying a chair which he had filched from somewhere, so that they could sit together.

'They can't tell a lot until she comes round, but they think she will be all right,' he said. 'The X-rays show a fracture of the skull, but it's only a crack; that will heal up of its own accord in time, though she'll have to be careful for a few months.'

'What about her leg?' asked Paul. He kept remembering the first time he saw Joanna, pirouetting round the kitchen table to show off her ballet steps, and then seeing her again as she lay on the road.

'Oh, that's nothing to worry about,' said Mr Abraham. 'Children are always breaking arms and legs. They mend

76

very easily. Haven't you ever broken any bones?'

'No,' said Paul. He was sturdy and thickset, not the breaking kind.

'I have,' said Mr Abraham. 'Fell out of a tree when I was about your age. Broke both legs.'

'Did it hurt?'

'Yes. Agony. I remember it now. And there was a bull in the field. Nothing else – just me and the bull.'

'What happened?'

'The bull walked slowly over and snuffed at me with those great wide wet nostrils bulls have; and then he began to graze alongside me.'

'Had you climbed the tree to escape the bull?'

'No, not exactly. We lived in very flat country, in East Anglia. You only had to get up a little way and you could see for miles. I wanted to climb this tree – it was the tallest tree around, and stood on a little rise – because I thought I'd see a little bit further than I'd ever seen before. But it was in this field with the bull, and the farmer had a notice – Beware of the Bull. I expect it was just to scare us and keep us out of his field. It did scare me, too, but I was determined to climb that tree, so one day, when I thought the bull wasn't looking, I climbed the gate and ran across to the tree and up I went – and down I came.'

Paul thought about Mr Abraham in his tree; he imagined him looking just as he did now, only in those long baggy shorts and jackets he had seen in old school photographs. It reminded him of himself in the skylight he helped Mr Abraham to build as a lookout for UFOs on the roof of his old cottage.

'You still do like climbing things to see further, don't you?' he said.

'There's always something further to see,' said Mr Abraham. 'I expect Joanna's parents will be here soon, don't you?'

Paul knew that the hospital had telephoned them very

soon after Joanna had been admitted, and it was only to be expected that they would come up to London by the first train. But where was his mother? He did not want her here, but she lived in London and was supposed to be in charge of Joanna. He looked at Mr Abraham's watch. It said seven-thirty-five – three hours since the accident.

'There must be somewhere in a place of this size where one can get something to eat,' said Mr Abraham, catching the direction of Paul's glance and looking at his watch, as well. 'I expect you're hungry. Excuse me —' He got up and trotted after a passing nurse. Paul admired the way the old man refused to be quelled by his surroundings. He was not sure whether he was hungry, though he knew he was empty; he had a flat, sickish feeling inside him, and was not sure whether food would make it better or worse.

'The answer,' said Mr Abraham, returning, 'is that there is a hospital shop that sells all sorts of things, but it shuts at five-thirty; there's a much more intelligent person who sells hot dogs and such-like from a stall immediately outside one of the hospital gates all evening, but it would take at least a quarter of an hour to get there from here; there's a tea-machine and a chocolate machine in the casualty department, which would probably take almost as long to reach and hardly sounds worth it —'

'It isn't,' said Paul, who had seen quite enough of the casualty department.

' — or if you can settle for a cup of tea and a biscuit for the time being, the nurse will bring us one here.'

'It doesn't matter,' said Paul. 'I'm not hungry.'

'I'd like a cup of tea and a biscuit,' said Mr Abraham. 'I wish you would keep me company.'

While they drank their tea, Paul remembered to ask Mr Abraham why he had been coming to look for him.

'Oh, yes, that,' said the old man unhurriedly. 'Drink

up your tea, **Paul**, so as to give me a chance to finish mine. Once I start talking it'll get cold, and it seems such a waste.' So it was not until the hot sweet tea and the biscuit and the Mars bar that a passing woman in a dressing-gown gave him had all found their way into the hollow cold place inside Paul, and the sickish feeling was replaced by a warm glow, that Mr Abraham said, 'It was something to do with your father.'

'Oh, yes,' said Paul, levelly.

'Tell me what you know about him, so that I can go on from there.'

So Paul told him what he could remember about his father, and what he had been told by his grandparents; and after a little pause, what Joanna had said the night before. 'But,' he added, 'I expect he's dead, really.' He had worded it like a statement, but he could not prevent it from sounding like a question, and he looked up into Mr Abraham's face for the answer. The old judge looked gravely back at him. 'I'm not going to pretend anything, or hide anything,' he said, 'and I'll answer that when we come to it; but I think it is best to start at the beginning and take everything in order as it happened.'

'Yes,' said Paul. For a moment he was afraid, and wished it was Uncle William with him, who could be relied on to tell him nothing that wouldn't be totally harmless to hear.

'When your mother ran away,' said Mr Abraham, 'your father became ill. He had what is called a nervous breakdown, and took to drinking a lot.'

'I didn't know that.'

'He was a long-distance lorry driver, as you probably knew, and he lost his job because he had his driving licence taken away after he'd had an accident when he'd been drinking. Then he went away to some city – Liverpool I think it was – to try and get other work. He really tried, then, to give up drinking – that was the time you remember, when he used to come home and visit you.'

'Yes.'

'Then he got into worse trouble, I suppose because he couldn't get work and couldn't find anywhere to live, and he got in with a drug-taking crowd. He was still not well, really, in his mind. I don't know whether you can understand that – maybe we can talk about that later. Anyway, he became a real down-and-out, living on the streets, rough, you know, and spending all his money on drugs and drink, and not getting enough to eat. That's when he first stopped writing, or coming to see you. He couldn't afford to, and he was ashamed, too, I expect.'

'Yes,' said Paul. 'Nana didn't —' he searched in his mind for the old-fashioned phrase he had heard her use — 'she didn't hold with drink or anything like that. She used to go to Chapel, regular. And my dad did; he used to sing in all the concerts, Grandad said.' That last bit didn't fit, and he glanced at Mr Abraham to see what he thought.

'People don't always behave the way you might expect,' said Mr Abraham. 'I daresay your mother's relations were surprised when she married a poor Welsh farmer who sang in Chapel. Anyway, have you ever seen what they call a wino, Paul, or a drug-addict since you've been in London?'

'Yes,' said Paul. He thought of the old man, or so he had thought him to be, slumped in the street corner that first day, when his mother had been modelling and he had found the ice-cream shop. He had seen plenty more like him since then, flung like dirty overcoats in careless corners of the city, and had noticed that many of them, on closer inspection, were not old at all, just bleached and shapeless.

'One day he got picked up, more or less unconscious, by a group of kind people who belonged to some religious sect.'

80

'I know – the Salvation Army.' Paul had seen them around in their uniforms.

'No, not this time, though it often is. These people belonged to some group that started in America, very sincere people, I expect, but . . . we'll come to that in a minute. They got him to a hospital, and they visited him and helped him all through the time that he was in danger of dying – you see he was really very ill – and when he was ready to be discharged from hospital they took him into their community, and eventually he became a member of the group and has worked with them ever since.'

'You mean, he's still alive?'

'Yes, but he's living in America now.'

'But why . . . ?'

'Why didn't he write, or come and see you, when he got better?'

'He didn't even come when Nana died.'

'At the beginning, I don't think he could even remember who he was or where he had come from. And afterwards – this is the bit I think you may find difficult to understand. This religious community, you can only join it if you give up everything you had before, not just money, but your family, everything. Be born again, like the Bible says.'

'Where is he now?'

'In America, living in one of their communities there. That's why the authorities took so long to trace him. There was the question of the farm, you see; unless he could be proved dead, he would be the owner – is the owner, in fact. Only he wants to sell it; the money is supposed to go to the community. He has to do that, you see; he has to give everything to them. Only I think in fact the law will see that most of the money goes into paying for your upkeep.'

Paul shook his head. The money side wasn't his business. It was something else that hurt. 'You mean, he didn't write and find out about me – they found out about him?'

'Yes. That is so. But then, remember, he didn't know about your grandfather.'

'He does now, doesn't he?'

'Yes.'

'And he's staying with these people in America? He's not coming back, is he?'

'No, he can't do that, not unless he leaves the community.'

Paul folded the Mars bar wrapper into half, very carefully creasing it so that the edges came exactly together; then he folded it again, and creased again, and folded again. His mind did not register what his fingers were doing. All the time it took him to reduce the wrapper to a tiny half-inch square, he said nothing at all. The scrap of paper in his hand fidgeted him, and he got up and walked across to a pedal-bin just down the passage. He pressed the lever with his foot, dropped in the wrapper and let the lid come down again with a slam. Then he walked back to his chair and sat down.

'That's it, then,' he said.

'Paul. I don't know if I've done right. I've told it you all, and I've told it you straight, because I think any other way does more harm than good. I'm not sure your uncle and aunt would agree – and I wouldn't have chosen this place if I could have helped it. Hospital passages aren't very cheerful places.'

'It wouldn't have made any difference, being somewhere else.'

'It might, you know, it might. Do you remember . . . ?' He left the sentence unfinished, because a nurse came up to them.

'The little girl is coming round. Will you come and see her?' She spoke to Mr Abraham. 'Only one,' she added, as Paul got up. 'I'm afraid you'll have to wait here just a little bit longer.'

'She doesn't really know me,' said Mr Abraham. 'It's Paul she'll want to see. I'm only keeping the boy company until her parents arrive.' He pressed Paul firmly forwards, and though the nurse hesitated, she gave in. 'Just sit by her quietly,' she said, taking Paul into the ward and behind the curtains round the bed nearest the door. 'And don't worry if she doesn't say anything.'

Paul had been to visit his grandfather in the local cottage hospital, and this was not so very different, once he was out of the maze of corridors and into the ward itself. Joanna was stirring in the bed, but she opened her eyes several times before she really looked at Paul as though she recognised him.

'Here's your brother come to see you,' said the nurse brightly.

'Paul? Where's Mummy?'

'Coming,' said Paul. 'I've put your lucky button back in your coat pocket.'

'Did we ever get to the Angel?' He could not make out at first what she was talking about, and she had to repeat it.

'Something about angels, dear,' said the nurse. 'Tell her she doesn't need to worry about angels for a good few years.'

'Oh,' said Paul, remembering. 'No, but it doesn't matter. I'll go another day.'

She was turning her head from side to side, looking everywhere. 'My coat?'

Paul said, 'She wants to know where her coat is.'

'All your clothes are quite safe, dear. You won't need them for a little while. You just stay quietly in bed and get better.'

'She has something in her coat pocket she wants,' said Paul. The nurse opened the locker and showed her the

83

coat. 'Is it still there?' Joanna asked.

Paul felt in the pocket till he found the little metal object. 'It's there all right,' he said. 'Do you want it?'

'I gave it to you,' she said.

'You shouldn't have. I don't need luck like you seem to. Shall I leave it there?'

'Yes, please.' She closed her eyes for a while, opening them again to say, 'I think I can hear Daddy.'

Paul had heard his uncle's voice, too. 'I'd better go, then,' he said. Joanna did not answer. She was looking past him, through the gap in the curtains, at her parents coming into the room.

6

Outside, Mr Abraham said, 'The Ward Sister is just trying to contact your mother again, on the telephone.'

'There's no point her coming, now Auntie Jean's here,' said Paul.

'No, but she ought to know what's happened.' They stood by the open office door, while the Sister talked to Megan, occasionally breaking off to ask them something; then Mrs Dawkes was fetched from Joanna's bedside, to confirm some arrangement. Paul wanted to get away from the hospital now, but instead he was left dangling on the edge of other people's arrangements. His aunt paused after finishing the telephone conversation and before going back to Joanna.

'Paul, darling,' she said, 'are you all right?'

'Yes.'

'There's a Mr Holcombe coming to take you back to your mother's – do you know who I mean?'

'Yes.'

She looked at him, troubled. 'I'm not quite sure why Megan couldn't come and fetch you herself.'

'It doesn't matter.'

'Anyway, you've been hanging around this place long enough. High time you went home, to a good meal and bed. I can't understand what . . . never mind, we'll talk about it tomorrow. I must go back to Joanna now.'

Paul watched her go, and turned to Mr Abraham. 'I don't want to go back to Megan's,' he said.

Mr Abraham looked him up and down. 'No,' he said. He didn't say any more, and after a pause, Paul said, 'What do you mean, No?'

'I agree that you don't want to go to Megan's,' said the judge. 'I don't specially want to go back to my club, but

I'm too old to sleep out on the Embankment, and you're too young. The police would pick you up, and I'd get bronchitis.'

'I'm not going,' said Paul. Somewhere at the back of his mind he knew he was being childish and stupid and fighting a battle which he could never hope to win, but he did not care. 'Mr Holcombe can't make me.' He leant against the wall of the corridor and folded his arms.

Mr Abraham surveyed him in silence briefly, and then turned and knocked on the office door.

'Where are you going?' said Paul, suspiciously, but a voice had called 'Come in,' and Mr Abraham merely said, 'I'll tell you in a minute,' and disappeared inside. Paul wondered whether to run off, but having arrived in a service lift, he had no idea which way to go.

'That was all right,' said Mr Abraham, cheerfully, reappearing well within the minute he had allowed himself. 'I was just in time.'

'What were you doing? In time for what?'

'To catch your Mr Holcombe before he left. It would have been such a waste for him to have come here if you're not going back with him.'

Paul looked as bewildered as a boxer whose opponent has collapsed before he had hit him. 'Come on,' Mr Abraham went on, before Paul had time to speak. 'How do we get out of here? Ah, there.' He pointed to the words *Way Out* written over some swing doors. Soon they came to a flight of stairs and a lift, side by side.

'Which is quicker, I wonder?' said Mr Abraham, 'I know; you take the stairs, and I'll go in the lift; they're bound to come out in the same place.'

'How many stairs are there?' asked Paul.

'I've no idea. Nor do I know how long I shall have to wait for the lift. I bet you a hot dog at the hot dog stall that I'll get there first.'

'Bet you won't,' said Paul. As he trotted down the

zigzag flights, he reflected that he had better win, for he had no money to buy Mr Abraham a hot dog. Not that he'll mind, he thought, but he saw the lift slide by on its way up, and heard it stop, and ran faster than ever.

He got there first, easily, with time enough to run off out into the street, but he didn't. Curiosity had taken the edge off his angry determination; he wanted to know what the judge had in mind.

Mr Abraham had food in mind. 'I've been thinking,' he said. 'You've probably been living on bread all day. I've got a better idea. Have you ever seen the river at night?'

'No,' said Paul. He had, however, seen an awful lot of London, today especially, and a bit more of it – even the river at night – was a poor substitute for a meal.

He had done his companion an injustice. Mr Abraham hailed a taxi, and they sped through the lighted streets.

'Where are we going?' said Paul. He did not like to ask if Mr Abraham was taking him to spend the night with him. Instead, he said, 'What did you mean about sleeping at your club?' To Paul, clubs were things you joined, not places to stay.

Mr Abraham said, 'A London club is like a kind of zoo for species that are in danger of becoming extinct; old generals, and old judges, sit about in large leather chairs and men dressed like penguins bring them things to eat at feeding time. The only difference is that the public are never allowed in, and —' he paused and glanced at Paul — 'I'm afraid boys are never allowed to sleep there. Now, there's rather a handy take-away place just down here.' He directed the taxi-driver down an alley and asked him to wait. 'Do you like Chinese food?'

'I don't know,' said Paul. 'I shouldn't think so.'

'Then I should stick to chicken and chips,' said Mr Abraham. 'Too many new things in one day is a mistake.'

They climbed back into the taxi five minutes later with

two cartons of soup, a large packet of chicken and chips, two ice-creams in tubs and a can of orangeade and set off again. After a short drive, they got out once more. Mr Abraham paid off the taxi-driver, and led Paul down some steps and round a corner. Before them lay the Thames, arched by jewelled bridges. Between the crescents of mirrored lights the water glittered blackly. The tall buildings, dark against the city's perpetually orange sky, stood respectfully back, as though shouldered casually away by the kingly river, so that Paul felt a country-like spaciousness around him, There were benches, some of them already booked for the night by London's homeless, but Mr Abraham led the way to an empty one.

'Soup,' he said. 'Though you might like to eat the chicken first, if the soup is too hot for you.'

'Aren't you having any chicken and chips?'

'No, thank you. There are some things you don't seem to enjoy so much as you get older; but then, other things you appreciate more – like sitting on a bench on a lovely warm evening, and hot soup. And perhaps some things don't hurt so much, either.'

Paul said, 'Why can't I have ordinary parents like other children?'

'Seekers,' said Mr Abraham. 'Always looking for perfection. Your mother too, I suppose, in her way. Do you think your father found that dreams gave him a feeling of the power of God that he had looked for in the village Chapel, and then in your mother, and not found? But really truly you have to earn your dreams if they're going to be any good to you – if you try and drink them, or smoke them, or inject yourself with them, they can poison you.' He tipped the plastic mug to drain the last of the soup, and sighed. 'Do you think your father's found a better way than that now, Paul?'

'But what about me?'

88

'Yes. You're right, Paul. There's something wrong there. What is it? Do you know, the longer I live, the more questions I ask and the fewer answers I can give.' He peeled the top off the ice-cream tub. 'It's a long time since I ate an ice-cream like this, on a bench, with a plastic shovel. One thing, Paul. Don't bury your father. He's no use to you at the moment – maybe that's not his fault. But one day you'll get to know him, and he'll get to know you. That's something to keep at the back of your mind while you grow up as part of Joanna's family.'

Paul said, staring at the black water, 'I don't belong to Joanna's family.'

'Belong?' exclaimed Mr Abraham. 'Of course you don't belong. Only belongings belong. Mind you, some people act as though they're only belongings, expecting someone else to be responsible for whatever happens to them, but not you, Paul. You don't wait to be told what to do with yourself.'

'You know what I mean,' said Paul. Joanna knew, he thought. She had understood what he meant about belonging.

'I said, part of, not belonging,' said Mr Abraham. 'Your shoes belong to you. You'd find it annoying to lose them, but you could always get another pair. But your foot is part of you; you'd miss your foot a lot more than your shoe.'

'I'm not part of Joanna's family like that. They don't miss me; they wouldn't have pushed me off to London while they—' he remembered that they hadn't gone to Spain after all – 'for the holidays.'

Mr Abraham licked out the last of his ice-cream. 'I wonder if you're right about that. I've got a kind of feeling there may have been other reasons for that, but that's not my business. But you know, you've not been there very long, and growing new parts takes time. And it takes longer as you get older, so it will take longer for your

89

uncle and aunt than for you and Joanna.'

'I don't mind Auntie Jean, but Uncle William . . .'
He left the sentence unfinished, because none of the ex-
pressions he had heard boys use about grown-ups, their
fathers or teachers or neighbours, seemed to fit. His
feeling about Uncle William went deeper than that.
'Anyway, that isn't the point. Perhaps they don't want me
back, ever. They don't have to, do they? They can push
me off on Megan and Mr Holcombe.'

'I don't know who this Mr Holcombe is, but I'm
beginning to feel very sorry for him,' said the judge. 'It
seems to me he gets the muddy end of every stick.'

'That's why I don't want to go back there tonight. I
don't want them to think Megan's place is my place, because it isn't. I'd rather have no place at all. I hate it
there, I hate it, I hate it!' The last bit took Paul himself
by surprise; it suddenly welled up in his mind from some
place he knew nothing of, and got swallowed in an up-
rush of ridiculous sobs. After a few moments, he added,
in a small, dismal voice, 'Auntie Jean would have put five
pence under my pillow, and then Joanna wouldn't have
got run over.'

Mr Abraham pondered this piece of information for a
few minutes and decided to let it alone. 'Of course,' he
said. 'Tell me, supposing it was you who got run over.
Where would Joanna spend the night?'

'At Megan's, I suppose.'

'And if you were lying ill in a hospital bed, and your
aunt and uncle wanted to be with you but they couldn't,
because Joanna made a fuss about staying at Megan's,
how would you feel?'

'Cross, I suppose,' said Paul. He sighed. 'Oh, damn,'
he said.

'It can be damnable, being part of a family, sometimes,' said Mr Abraham.

Paul drained the last of the orangeade. 'Are you going

to ring up and ask Mr Holcombe to come here and fetch me?' he asked, with a small grin.

'No,' said the judge. 'I'll take you there by taxi. We will be kind to poor Mr Holcombe.'

Megan was all gratitude to Mr Abraham, and affection for Paul and concern about Joanna when they got back to the flat. Mr Holcombe explained he had just been waiting till Paul came back, and now he must be on his way, and could he give His Honour a lift to his club? Mr Abraham accepted with grave politeness, but there was a twinkle in his eye when he turned to say goodbye to Paul.

'Where did he spring from?' asked Megan, as soon as they had gone.

'He's somebody we know in Wales,' said Paul. 'He is buying Grandad's cottage.' Megan still looked perplexed, but Paul could not face telling her what Mr Abraham had really come about. Now the others had gone, Megan was at a loss, as usual, about what part to play, and Paul felt too tired to bother with her. 'Can I go straight to bed?' he said. 'I've had heaps to eat.'

He was truly tired and slept on the settee until well into the morning. Megan had moved into Joanna's little room, so that Auntie Jean and Uncle William could have the use of her larger one when they eventually came in from the hospital. Paul heard nothing of their comings and goings in the night, but when he awoke it was to the sound of crockery chinking in the kitchen next door. It wasn't very loud, or frequent, and there were no voices so presumably only one person was in there. Paul blinked in the bright sunlight, and wondered who it was, while yesterday's events gradually took shape in his mind. He could tell from the sun it was late, past the time his mother usually went out. Perhaps it was Auntie Jean.

He rolled off the couch and went through into the kitchen, in bare feet and pyjamas. Uncle William was

91

sitting at the kitchen table, also in pyjamas, drinking a cup of coffee. He looked as tousled as Paul, and unshaved.

'Oh, sorry,' said Paul, and backed away. He was sure Uncle William would not want to be seen like that. At home, he was always up and dressed before the children got up, during the week, and at weekends made sure they were safely downstairs before going to the bathroom.

'Don't go away,' said Uncle William. 'Don't you want some breakfast?'

'Shall I get dressed first?'

'Oh. Oh, yes.' His uncle looked down at himself, as though surprised to realise his own state of undress. 'I'd better do the same, hadn't I?' He drank up the remains of his coffee. 'I'm afraid your mother has had to go out, and Auntie Jean has gone back to the hospital to see Joanna, so there's only me here.' Paul could see he was trying to be friendly, but felt ill at ease, as always, at having to talk directly to his nephew.

'How is she?' he asked. That he must know before letting his uncle escape.

'Better,' said Uncle William. 'Should be all right now. She'll have to stay where she is for a few days, and then she can come home.'

Paul wanted to say, 'What about me?' but instead he said, 'I'll go and get dressed.'

He expected to have finished breakfast comfortably before his uncle reappeared, because it only took him two minutes to get into jeans and tee-shirt and he knew it would take Uncle William a lot longer than that. However, his uncle must have hurried because he came back into the kitchen, tightening his tie, while Paul was still frying sausages.

'You look very competent,' he said. Paul could think of no reply, so he said, 'Would you like some?'

'No, thank you. I've had all I want except another cup of coffee, to keep you company.'

92

'You don't need to,' said Paul. 'I always have breakfast on my own.'

'It seems to me you've been doing most things on your own since you've been in London.'

'Yes.'

'What exactly were you doing all day yesterday? How did you come to be right up near Kilburn when the accident happened? Your mother said she thought you were playing in the Park.'

'It was my fault,' said Paul, heavily. 'We got lost.' He looked up at his uncle. 'She never said anything about the Park to us. She never bothers where I go so long as I come home in the evenings and don't leave dirty dishes in the sink.' His uncle still said nothing, so after swallowing another mouthful of sausage, he added, 'It gets dull, playing in the Park every day, and anyway Joanna wanted to see Buckingham Palace.'

'That's a long way from Kilburn.'

'It was because of the Monopoly board, too.' Paul explained about that, and then outlined their wanderings around London the previous day. At first it seemed funny having his uncle as a listener, but Mr Dawkes kept so quiet that after a bit Paul forgot about him being his uncle. He remembered, however, when Mr Dawkes looked at his watch. He broke off, and said, 'Are you waiting to go back to the hospital? I can wash up and that.'

'No,' said Uncle William. 'I've got to catch a train back to Port Mynach at twelve o'clock, but there's things I've got to tell you about first.'

Paul's mouth went dry. 'I'm to live with my mother. I'm not to come back,' he muttered.

Mr Dawkes appeared not to have heard straightaway, but the words caught up with him just as he was about to speak, and he checked himself.

'Is that what your mother has told you?' he asked.

'No, of course not. She doesn't want me. But if you

93

don't, then she's got to, hasn't she?'

'And what do you want?'

'It doesn't make much difference what I want, does it?'

Mr Dawkes got up and wandered round the room, 'Put it this way,' he said. 'Would you mind very much coming back to live with us?'

Paul stared at him, too surprised to say anything. If Mr Dawkes had looked at his face, he would have known Paul's answer, but he was finding the conversation much too difficult to do that. He wiped the steam from the window and looked out at the uninteresting view. With his back to Paul, he said, 'I'm sorry about all the things that went wrong when you came to live with us. It was my fault, some of it . . . I'm sorry.'

Paul still did not say anything; he did not know how to begin to talk to this different uncle.

Mr Dawkes wandered on, straightening a saucepan lid, rearranging the things on the table. 'What I thought was, well, it must be pretty lonely for you here, and you and Joanna seem to get on all right together, and your aunt is . . . that is, both of us are . . . very fond of you, Paul. . . .'

'Don't,' said Paul. 'Of course I like it better with you than being here. Only I thought . . . I thought, what with running away and – well, I'm not really your business, am I . . . ?' This conversation was so odd, and difficult, that Paul broke off and said, 'How's Prickles?'

Mr Dawkes smiled, as though one hurdle had been safely cleared, and sat down again opposite Paul. 'Very well,' he said. 'Eating all the slugs.'

Paul got up to take his plate to the sink, but his uncle said, 'Sit down a minute, Paul. There's something else I've got to tell you.'

Paul sat down again, easy now, sure that nothing could be as surprising as the new uncle he had been discovering.

Mr Dawkes cleared his throat. He said, 'This isn't easy to say.' He cleared his throat again and looked at his watch, as though wondering whether there was time to put off what he was going to say a little longer. Evidently there was not, for he suddenly looked Paul full in the eyes, with a very odd expression on his face, and said, 'I'm going to have to go to prison.'

Paul stared at him; he thought at first it must be some kind of joke and did not know what to say, in case it was, or in case it wasn't. He wished Joanna were here; she understood her father's peculiar sense of humour; he also wished his uncle would stop staring at him, because he could not keep the confusion out of his face.

'Is it a joke?' he said at last.

'No. It's true.' Still his uncle stared at him. Things nagged at Paul's memory, references to his uncle and aunt being in some kind of trouble, even something Mr Abraham had said yesterday to which he had paid little attention. But there was another, quite different kind of memory which for a moment he could not place. Then it came to him. The young man whose van had knocked Joanna down had stared at him in just that way, looking for . . . what? Blame? Pity? Company in an awful moment of loneliness?

'Prison?' he said. 'Why?'

'I haven't told anyone, except Jean, of course. She knows.' The 'Auntie', always so carefully remembered, had gone; Paul was the listener, not the little boy. 'I haven't told Joanna yet. We didn't want either of you to have to know. I thought perhaps it wouldn't happen, but I can see now that was stupid.'

'Perhaps it won't happen,' said Paul.

'I'm afraid it will.' He put on an air of mock jollity for a moment. 'Just the place for a wicked uncle, eh?'

'No,' said Paul, unsmiling. The response seemed to steady Mr Dawkes and he found his way back into himself.

'It's going to be worse for Joanna than for you – do you understand?'

'Yes,' said Paul. 'You're her father. Not that I don't mind,' he explained. Did he mind? It was all so strange, so peculiar. 'But Joanna will mind more.'

'That's why we need you at home. To keep Joanna company, and your aunt. The man about the house. . . .' He fumbled for the familiar patronising joke.

He still had not answered Paul's question. 'But why . . . ?' Paul began, and stopped because it sounded rude to be questioning one's uncle like a criminal.

'I know,' said Uncle William. 'It's a long story.' He sighed, and paused, as though thinking back to the beginning of that long story. Then he told Paul how he had always wanted to have a nice house and a nice garden, and two cars, one for each of them, and plenty of money to buy things for his wife and Joanna, but though he had a good steady income with the insurance company, it did not seem to bring in enough money to pay for all the things he wanted. 'If you work in an insurance office,' he said, 'you are dealing with thousands of pounds – millions, sometimes – every day. You get to think that a thousand pounds would make an awful lot of difference to you, but the company wouldn't miss it. And then you think of how it could be done; it's quite difficult, actually, because of all the accounts and things, but I found out how it could be done, along with a man I knew who looked after the insurance for a big factory. We worked it between us that we shared a thousand pounds a year between us; then it got a bit more, and a bit more. I knew it was risky, and we were bound to be found out, but my partner wouldn't let me pull out. And then, of course, they did find out.'

'How?' said Paul. It was all a bit mysterious to him, but Uncle William had paused and Paul felt he must say something.

96

'Oh, either my firm got to wonder why this particular factory wasn't paying much insurance, or the factory bosses began to wonder why they were paying so much, and they got together over it without consulting me or my partner and they found that all this money was going out of the factory accounts and never coming into the insurance company's accounts. So then they came to see me – and him.'

'So then what happened?'

'Then we got taken to court, where we've been busy inventing stories to explain it all away. We've got very good lawyers, and I hoped that if I just kept on denying everything, the jury would believe me and maybe put all the blame on the other man and find me Not Guilty.'

'Perhaps they will.'

'That's what I've been hoping. Jean – Auntie Jean – I don't think, now I look back, ever really agreed, but she backed me up. Every day, in court, I've been answering this question and that, trying to make everything fit. But it was all lies, Paul, do you see?'

He looked at Paul with that same searching look, and sighed again, as though disappointed at seeing only a round-faced boy opposite him. 'I don't know why I'm telling you this, only there's no one else. I mean, lots of people *know*, of course; it's all been reported in the local newspapers and television, but as long as I keep pretending I haven't done anything wrong, they have to keep pretending, too. People avoid talking to me, and when they can't avoid it, they talk about the weather. That's why Joanna was staying with her grandparents, and then came up here. At least it doesn't make the national news.'

Paul said, 'Then you still don't know? I mean, if they'd found you guilty, you wouldn't be here now, would you?'

'I rang up my lawyer this morning and told him to alter my plea from "Not Guilty" to "Guilty". You know what I mean, do you?'

Paul nodded. 'Why?'

Uncle William didn't answer for a moment. Then he said, 'Because I'm sick of the whole business of telling lies. Because any fool could see I wasn't going to get away with it, and I'll probably get a shorter sentence for owning up. Because it was a long journey up to London last night, just me and your Auntie Jean, not knowing whether Joanna was going to live, or might be injured for life, and – well, if you want something badly enough, you feel you're more likely to get it if you pay something big, a sort of bargain with God. I can't tell you what was the real reason – you must decide that for yourself.'

Paul looked at his uncle, then shifted his gaze to the patch of sky visible through the grimy pane of glass wiped free of steam. 'I'll look after the garden for you while you're in prison,' he said. 'Will it be for long?'

'A year? Two years? Something like that, the lawyer said. But you see, we'll have to sell the house. It's not just that there'll be no more of that money, and there'll be legal expenses to pay, but I'll lose my job. Insurance companies can't employ people who have been sent to prison for corruption and fraud.'

'I – I'm sorry,' said Paul. He found he did mind, after all, about Uncle William. Then another thought struck him. 'Will I – will you be able to afford to have me? Mr Abraham said there'll probably be some money for me from Grandad's cottage; and I can do holiday jobs.'

'Oh, we'll manage. There's family allowance and things. If we move back down into the town, near where we lived before, we won't need a car. But if Auntie Jean gets a job, which she says she will, it will mean you and Joanna will have to look after yourselves more than we've let you in the past.'

'Suits me,' said Paul, with a grin.

'Yes,' said Mr Dawkes. 'I rather fancy it will. You'll have to teach Joanna to fry sausages. And we'll have a little

98

garden – big enough for Prickles. You'll have to keep that in order.'

'That's easy,' said Paul. His uncle was standing staring out of the window again, and Paul was reminded of a man locked in a prison cell, looking out on a little square of bright world. 'Those things don't matter,' he said. 'Cars and that – I never had none of all that before I came to live with you. But prison – that's different. How often can we come and see you?'

Uncle William turned to face him and smiled. 'I don't know. Often, I expect.' He looked at his watch. 'Auntie Jean should be back any time now; she's coming to see me off at Paddington, to wish me luck.'

'Why have you got to go back today? You were coming up for the day today anyway.'

'Yes, but that was when I was still pleading "Not Guilty". But now I've changed it there doesn't have to be a jury, just a judge to pass sentence, and he may hear the end of my case this afternoon, if I get back in time.'

'Then you'll know this evening?'

'May not; he may wait till tomorrow to decide the sentence.'

'Isn't Auntie Jean going with you?'

'I think she ought to stay here with Joanna, don't you?'

Paul thought of Uncle William all alone in the house, with only Prickles for company, coming back from the court and wondering all evening and all night what the judge would say, and having to talk to the neighbours about the weather.

'No,' he said. 'I can stay with Joanna, and Auntie Jean can go back with you.'

'How would you manage? I mean, your mother never seems to be here; and I'm not sure whether the hospital would let you.'

'They let me yesterday; if there's no one else they'd let me; and I'm quite used to Megan not being here. I know all the visiting hours; I had plenty of time to read them yesterday while I was waiting. Auntie Jean's here, anyway.' Paul, more accustomed to the noises in the block of flats than his uncle, had caught the sound of the lift stopping on the landing outside. He went to let her in.

'Hullo, Paul,' she said. 'Joanna sent you her love. She's down in the theatre now, having her leg set.' She turned to her husband. 'I saw the surgeon. He said it was a very simple break, and there should be no problems. In fact, there's no reason why she shouldn't come home tomorrow, if we could have had the car here by then, and then she can attend at our own hospital as an out-patient until it's healed. They're so short of beds here, I think they'd be glad to be rid of her, but they agreed to keep her an extra day or two when I explained we hadn't got the car here. Probably cheaper than sending her all the way to Wales in an ambulance.'

She was talking fast and nervously, but eventually her voice ran out in the silence. They all stood for a few moments without speaking, the three of them, in the London flat that was home to none of them. Then Uncle William said, 'I have been telling Paul everything.'

'Oh,' said Mrs Dawkes. She seemed to be wondering how much was 'everything'. 'And what does Paul think?'

'I think,' said Paul, 'that you should go back on the train with Uncle William and come back with the car tomorrow after . . . after . . .'

'After the sentence has been passed,' said Uncle William.

'And I can go and see Joanna this afternoon.'

'She probably won't have come round from the operation till this evening; they said to ring up about three. When does your mother get home?'

'I never know, but that doesn't matter. I can take a taxi if – if you can afford it. I could probably walk. I've got a map.' He went to get it.

'Oh dear,' said Auntie Jean. 'I want to be in two places at once. I don't know what's best to do.' She looked questioningly at her husband, but it was obviously not fair to ask him.

Paul said, 'Having a broken leg is nothing. Mr Abraham fell out of a tree into a field with a bull in it and broke both legs when he was my age.'

'Oh, Paul,' said Auntie Jean. 'If the nurses hadn't been telling me how marvellous you were last night, waiting and waiting and sticking with Joanna through thick and thin and not making any fuss, I'd say you were most unsympathetic.'

Paul thought that was a funny way to look at it. 'I didn't have much choice,' he remarked. He had expected Joanna's parents to blame him for having let her get run over, but neither of them seemed to do that, not even Uncle William. It was Megan they blamed for that. 'Anyway, I know my way to the ward now, and they know me there, so I expect they'll let me see her.' He could not think why the grown-ups were being so dithery. It was all quite clear to him. 'I'd much rather be Joanna at this moment than Uncle William,' he said. 'After all, she's over the worst part, or will be when she comes round; Uncle William's still got his to come.'

'No,' said Uncle William. 'I'm over the worst part, too.' He paused, and then added, 'I think.'

'That settles it,' said Auntie Jean. 'I shall leave Joanna to you, Paul. I'm sure Megan will come with you, but just in case she can't, give him the money for a taxi, Will. I shall ring up the hospital around three, from Port Mynach station and then telephone you here, to tell you what the position is. Remember, Joanna knows nothing of all this business —' not having been with her husband and Paul during their conversation she could not quite bring herself to say clearly what the 'business' was —'and so don't say anything about it. I'll tell her myself tomorrow; I think that's best.'

'She'll wonder what has made you rush off,' said Paul.

'Tell her Auntie Jean's gone home to fetch the car,' said Uncle William. The old glibness still came naturally to him, but when he caught Paul's eye he added, a little self-consciously, 'It *is* true.'

'All right,' said Paul. The grown-ups were hustling about now, particularly Auntie Jean, who had not planned to be leaving, getting their belongings together. Uncle William gave Paul five pounds. 'You may not want all that,' he said. 'But if you need it, use it. Get some sweets for Joanna – she'll like that. And just in case your mother doesn't come home in time, do you know how to get a taxi?'

'You walk to the edge of a pavement and wave an umbrella,' said Paul, with memories of Mr Abraham. He would have gone back to Wales earlier this morning, which was a pity, but it couldn't be helped.

Auntie Jean wavered. 'I don't like to leave you wandering about London by yourself,' she said.

'I've been doing it for weeks,' said Paul. 'Anyway, I don't need a taxi. I can walk.' He had found the hospital in his London guide, and was tracing the streets with his finger. 'So I won't need all that money.'

'Keep it in case,' said his uncle. 'And if you don't need it, keep it for your birthday. September, isn't it? I shan't have a fiver to give you by then.'

'Oh dear,' said Auntie Jean. She looked as if she might cry.

There was one thing Paul had to ask. 'When do I come back?' he said.

'Tomorrow,' said Auntie Jean. 'With Joanna. I shan't be able to manage without you.'

'The day after tomorrow,' said Uncle William. 'I'm not having you driving both ways in one day. Besides, I hope you'll be in court with me tomorrow morning. You'll both have to stay tomorrow night here – if Megan will have you.'

'We are rather taking advantage of her,' said Auntie Jean.

'Don't worry,' said Paul. 'She'd much rather have you for two nights than me for ever.'

'That sounds hard. Do you feel that bad?'

'No,' said Paul. 'She's got Mr Holcombe, and I – I've got you.'

'We'll miss that train,' said Uncle William. He shook Paul by the hand and said, 'Come and see me soon.' Then the door shut behind them.

7

Paul neither had to walk to the hospital nor take a taxi, because the message his aunt gave him from the hospital was that he should not go to see Joanna before six o'clock, and by then Megan was home, and took him. She was picturing herself as the attentive aunt and mother, and a bit narked, too, Paul thought. 'Very odd, Jean going off again like that at the last minute,' she said. 'She'd said last night that William would have to go back but she'd stay on.'

'She's gone to fetch the car up,' said Paul. He didn't know what Megan knew about the family circumstances, but he remembered she had made a remark a week or so ago which showed she suspected something was up, and he did not want to have to talk about it with her.

'You'd think they'd tell me what was happening,' she said. 'After all, it is my flat. And how was I to know they'd both gone off and left you on your own?'

'We didn't know where to get hold of you,' said Paul. Doesn't she realise? he thought. She must know it's all a game of pretend. But it seemed she didn't, for after a moment she went on in the same slightly irritated, self-righteous tone, 'It was so annoying that I've been so tied up these last couple of days. They must think I'm never at home. I've scarcely seen Jean.'

'She'll be back tomorrow evening,' said Paul. He took an anxious breath. 'And then we all go back together the next day, so long as Joanna is well enough.' He couldn't imagine that his mother would object, but just suppose that she did. But she just looked at him rather sharply, and said nothing for a long time. When she referred to the matter again, they were on the bus. She said, 'You remember what Mr Holcombe said, about coming to stay sometimes at the pub, when we're settled in?'

'Yes,' said Paul.

'It's best that way. Best for all of us.'

'Yes,' said Paul.

Joanna was surprised to see Paul and not her mother, but she was cheered by the reason Paul gave for it, and by the sweets, though she did not eat any, which surprised Paul. She just kept wanting drinks of orange juice, a jug of which was by her bed. 'When will Mummy be back?' she asked.

'Tomorrow afternoon, about tea-time,' said Paul.

'Can you come and see me in the morning?'

Paul shook his head. 'I'm not allowed then,' he said. 'It's not visiting hours.'

'Mummy was here this morning.'

'That was special, because you were going to have your operation.'

'Can't I be special again tomorrow?' She asked a nurse about it, with her best smile, but hospital staff are not so easily wheedled as fathers.

There did not seem much to say; Joanna was tired, and Paul was full with news he must not tell her, and Megan kept looking at her watch. But Paul was accustomed to sitting quietly by his grandfather's bedside, and did so now. Joanna's eyes closed, and he thought she had gone to sleep. Megan signed to him that they should go, but Joanna suddenly opened her eyes again and said, 'Have you got a kite?'

'A kite?' said Paul, wondering if she was in a dream.

'I could see kites out of the window earlier.'

Paul looked out at the jumble of roofs and office blocks. 'I expect it was a pigeon,' he said.

'No, stupid, they were kites. Two of them, with streamers, over those houses.'

'From the Park, I expect,' said Megan. 'It's not far, as the crow flies.'

105

'Or the kite,' said Paul.

'I just thought, if you had a kite, you could fly it out there tomorrow morning and I'd know you were there.'

'I know where I can buy a kite,' said Paul.

'Are they very expensive?'

'Not really.' He could buy one with the unspent taxi money. 'I'd like to have a kite. We can fly it on the beach at home when your leg is better.'

'Will you, Paul? Will you get one and fly it so that I can see it from my window tomorrow morning?'

'I'll try. But I mightn't be able to get it to fly, or perhaps there'll be no wind, or it will be blowing in the wrong direction, or I'll be flying it in a bit of sky you can't see.'

'It's that bit,' said Joanna.

'Thanks,' said Paul. 'That's very helpful.'

'Try,' said Joanna. 'I'll be watching all morning. It's very lonely here.' Paul looked round the ward; there were at least a dozen other children, at this time mostly with their own relations with them. 'It doesn't look lonely,' he said. 'You haven't been here very long, and most of that time you've either been unconscious, or sleeping, or being operated on. I bet tomorrow I'll be flying my kite all morning and you'll forget to look because you'll be so busy talking.'

Joanna brightened, and looked sideways down the ward. 'Do you think I will?' she said hopefully. 'Perhaps you're right.' The prospect of making new friends always excited her; she made friends very easily. 'Do you think I'll feel better in the morning?' she asked Megan.

'I'm sure you will,' said Megan. 'Joanna's tired now, Paul. I think we ought to leave her to sleep.'

'I'll still be watching for the kite, though. I'll be able to tell everyone, "That's my kite." '

'It'll probably be someone else's,' said Paul. 'I can't tell all the other kite-fliers to take theirs down. Mine won't be

106

a very big one – they cost too much. I'll get a bird one, as big a bird one as I can, and I'll fly it, if I can, at half past eleven.'

'I'll be watching,' said Joanna.

Paul set off to buy his kite at nine o'clock the next morning, and took it straight into the Park at Marble Arch. He had never flown a kite in his life, but he had spent a good deal of his time recently watching other people, and he had a pretty good idea how to set about it. He had two hours in which to practise, and to work his way westwards to the area which, from studying his map, he reckoned lay under the right bit of sky. There wasn't a lot of wind, and it was trying to rain. The gaudy plastic bird flopped and flapped sullenly on its tether, rising unwillingly a few feet into the air in response to Paul's tugs, and then dashing itself into the ground. He ran, towing the petulant thing, until his legs ached and sweat poured from him. Then he sat down disconsolately on a park bench to unravel the sodden knotted thread.

'It ain't no use in this wet, love,' said an old woman at the other end of the bench. 'You better go home and come back when it's stopped this drizzle.'

'It's not much,' said Paul. 'And it's plastic. It says on the packet it'll fly in the rain.'

'You don't want to believe them things,' said the old woman. 'It's the string, see. You feel it – it's all heavy, isn't it? Been dragging on the wet grass, I know that.'

'You can't help it doing that,' said Paul.

'That's what I'm saying. You let the string dry out, and come again when the sun is shining, and it'll fly like a bird.'

'It *is* a bird,' said Paul.

'So it is,' said the old lady. 'A bird on a string, though. We never had none of those fancy things when we were kids. Used to make our own.'

'Did you used to fly kites, then?' said Paul. She sat shapeless as a squashed pear on the bench and the feet below the wrinkled stockings were gnarled and twisted as ancient pear-tree roots.

'Loved it, we did, when we were kids.'

'Where did you fly your kites?'

'Here, of course; here in the Park. There ain't nowhere else, except maybe Hampstead Heath, and that was too far saving only once or twice.'

'Have you always lived in London?'

'All my life. You haven't, have you? You're Welsh, aren't you?'

'Yes.'

'I've never been to Wales, but we used to reckon our kites went there.'

'How do you mean?'

'Well, when our kites got a little way up, we'd say, "Now we can see the King in Buckingham Palace" – Edward the Seventh, that was. Then they'd go up a bit further, and we'd say, "Now we can see Windsor Castle." Then it was the sea, the white cliffs of Dover. Mind, we didn't have television in those days, just school books and picture postcards. Then it would be Wales, or Scotland, or Ireland. All the furthest away places we could think of. India, China, and all. I been to the moon long before them astronauts got around to it. Do you think I'm talking rubbish?'

'No,' said Paul. 'Sort of – where the rainbow ends.'

'Better than that. Where the rainbow *begins*. Beginnings are better than endings.'

'It's the same thing, really,' said Paul. 'Depends which way you look at it.'

'Ah,' said the old woman. 'I weren't never too keen on grubbing for that old crock of gold. It was up the rainbow for me. But you can't get nowhere with a wet string. You need a bit of luck as well as a bit of imagination.'

'I've got to get it up this morning,' said Paul. He told her about Joanna in hospital, waiting to be visited by his bird.

'Well, now,' said the old lady, 'the sun's come out, that's one thing.'

'But the string's still wet.'

'You can't have it all your own way. Given one bit of luck, we'll make the next bit ourselves.'

'How?'

'What you want to do is, you want to unwind all that thread, and wind it up again the other way; I'll lay odds you haven't had more'n a quarter of it out yet, have you?'

'Not so much,' said Paul. 'Why don't I just cut it off?'

'Well of course, you could; but then you'd never see those Welsh hills of yours, would you?'

'I only need to get it high enough for Joanna to see.'

'Oh, well, if that's all you want. . . . I'd have thought you was the kind that wanted more'n that. But then, you ain't never flown a kite, have you?'

'No.'

'I'll tell you, then. When your kite goes up, your heart goes up; the higher the kite goes, the higher you go, too. However long your bit of string, it's never long *enough*. You always want to go further.'

Paul began to unwind his string in loops on the grass. 'That's like Mr Abraham,' he said.

'Here,' said the old woman. 'You'll get in a proper bundle of guts like that. Give us here.' She took the end and wound a few lengths from one outstretched hand to the other, as though she were winding wool. The spool spun and jiggled in Paul's hands, till all the string was looped between the old woman's hands. She gave a deft twist so that the inside of the skein rolled round to the outside, and nodded to Paul to take the first end, tucked tidily under her thumb. 'Your turn now,' she said. 'Wind away.'

109

It took longer to roll up the thread round the narrow spool again, and Paul began to get anxious about the passage of time, but all the while the sun shone down and dried the twinkles off the grass.

At last it was done, and he re-tied the end to his resting bird.

'I'll hold her for you,' said the old woman. She grasped the back of the bench and hauled her shapeless pear of a body up so that she was standing on the seat, her gnarled feet splayed across the bars. She noticed Paul glancing around, and said, 'Go on; there ain't nobody watching.' It was true; the Park had scarcely had time to fill up since the rain. Then she held the bright bird aloft. 'Get over there,' she said. 'Quick, before I fall off of this thing.'

Paul stepped backwards, letting the string unroll, until he was some twenty metres away. 'There's some wind coming,' he cried.

'Run, then'. Pull her up, pull her up! You got her! Don't stop now; keep jerking her.' She was standing on the bench, having released the bird, tugging an imaginary string as she watched the kite take uncertainly to the air in a series of looping lunges. 'Don't stop! Not till you feel the air take her. Whoops-a-daisy!' She put out a hurried hand to grip the back of the bench as she nearly over-balanced, and lowered herself ponderously to the ground.

'You all right?' called Paul, his eyes on his bird.

'Don't you fret about me. You just keep going. I'll watch your kite from here. I'll see when you get to where the rainbow begins!'

Her voice floated after him. The string was pulling steadily in his hands and his bird flew, at tree-top level. He stopped running and it stayed there, swinging a little from side to side, but no longer plunging. He let out a little string, and it dipped, but he jerked on the thread, and it rose up, higher than ever. Next time he let out the

110

string, the bird simply rose further away. The air had taken it, the warm living air from the hive that was London. Up it went, and up, and all the time Paul led it further and further west, till he reached the spot which he had marked down as being below the right bit of sky. From somewhere far away, over the hum of traffic, a clock chimed the half-hour. He was right on time.

With the eye of his bird, he looked in at the hospital window and saw Joanna, sitting up, making friends, showing off a bit, 'Look!' she was saying. 'There it is. That's my kite, come to see me.'

Somewhere his bird looked down on his mother, on Megan, sitting with one or other of her faces turned to the camera, or an audience; somewhere Mr Holcombe sat in an office, dreaming of his pub; he didn't suppose either of them would be looking up at his kite. Hunting crocks of gold. Funny, what the old lady had said. The rainbow didn't really have an end, when he came to think of it. You could waste your life away chasing it, and the gold it was supposed to lead you to. But they had beginnings, they must have, else they wouldn't be there. He knew how they happened, partly; his teacher had explained about prisms and refractions of light, and the mirrors of the eye. But how had these things come about? Sunlight and colours, and infinite space. And why?

He coaxed his kite higher, feeling the spool grow thinner in his hand. Now his bird could see Auntie Jean, speeding down the motorway, stretched like elastic between the people she loved. Would she see his bird? He would take her down on the beach, he and Joanna, when her day's work was finished, and show her how to fly a kite – but perhaps she already knew. That was something to find out, something round the corner.

His bird went higher. It looked down, down, on a grim building with narrow barred windows, hidden away behind a high wall. At one of those windows, the face of

Uncle William. Strange; a short time ago Paul would have said that Uncle William was the last person to be looking up to see his bird, up to the beginning of the rainbow. But now he must see it, for there was nothing else for him to look at, only a small square of sky.

'Look, Uncle William,' said Paul. 'Here's my kite, come to visit you.'

His kite looked down on Prickles, sleeping at this time of day in a dark corner; and on Grandpa in that other, faraway hospital.

He sent it up higher, to peer over the Cambrian hills and into the cottage tucked in a western fold. 'Hullo, Mr Abraham,' said Paul. He didn't stop to wonder if Mr Abraham was looking; he knew he would be.

Down the valley from the cottage stood the Chapel, guarding the graveyard where Grandad lay buried, and Nana too, but Paul did not send his bird there to look for them. They were at the cottage, in his memory; his grandmother hazy now, but Grandad bright and clear. The little clutch of grief inside his ribcage sent Paul's bird swinging sideways on the wind, to peer down at that smaller, newer graveyard, a patch of rank grass and a handful of long-withered flowers. Davy. Paul held the two griefs as steady in his heart as the tugging string in his hands. They hurt; not so much as once, but he knew there would always be a little hurt there, for the rest of his life. It was part of being Paul, just as the arc of the rainbow and the green valley were part of him.

He let the kite go further; now it was scarcely more than a dot in the sky, but straining upwards as strongly as ever. What could his bird see up there? Round the curve of the ocean, to America. Paul knew that his father would not be looking. He loosened his grip on the spool, to let his bird fly higher. It would not turn. He had come to the end of the thread. He stood on tiptoe to capture a few more centimetres.

112

'That's always the way it is,' said a voice behind him. The old woman had caught up with him and stood gazing up into the sky. 'Never mind. You've got a long way up, in spite of everything.'

'With a little help,' said Paul.

'Maybe,' said the old woman. 'Next time, you'll be wanting to put a longer string on her.'